Edwin Robertson was born in London, of Scottish parents, in 1912. He first studied physics, specializing in oils, and then read theology at Oxford. On ordination to the Baptist ministry he served churches in Luton and St Albans.

After the war he worked in the Religious Affairs Branch of the British Zone of Germany, and then became Assistant Head of Religious Broadcasting at the BBC, before becoming Study Secretary of the United Bible Societies (based in Geneva) and then Executive Director of the World Association for Christian Broadcasting.

Whilst retaining many international communication links, and his keen interest in the writings of Dietrich Bonhoeffer, as well as writing some seventy books himself, Edwin Robertson became Minister of Yeovil Baptist Church in Somerset and then of Westbourne Park Baptist Church in Paddington. He is currently Minister of Heath Street Baptist Church, Hampstead.

EDWIN ROBERTSON

Living Christianity

COLLINS
FOUNT PAPERBACKS

William Collins Sons & Co. Ltd
London • Glasgow • Sydney • Auckland
Toronto • Johannesburg

First published in Great Britain in 1990 by Fount Paperbacks

Fount Paperbacks is an imprint of
Collins Religious Division,
part of the Collins Publishing Group
8 Grafton Street, London W1X 3LA

Copyright © 1990 Edwin Robertson

Printed and bound in Great Britain by
William Collins Sons & Co. Ltd, Glasgow

For Lesley

CONTENTS

INTRODUCTION

There are two fundamental questions about Christianity: **Is it true?** and **Does it matter?** We may never be able to answer them to everybody's satisfaction, but in view of the claims Christianity makes and its survival over two thousand years, it would be frivolous to ignore them. We who live in a European culture have been so formed by the basic teaching of Christianity that we should want to know whether we have been nurtured on a lie.

Or, perhaps, the time of Christianity has passed? It was useful for a while as European culture evolved, but the Enlightenment and the Industrial Revolution and the growth of a Scientific World View have outgrown it. Is that what is true? That Christianity had its place and achieved remarkable feats in the childhood of our nations, but we have outgrown it, we need it no more? It doesn't really matter in the real world which lives by the cold light of science?

Karl Marx thought that. He had some hard things to say about religion as privilege, but he thought kindly of a Christianity which had been the consolation of the poor and oppressed. It allowed the poor to cry and to hope, even if their hope was pushed on to life after death. He did not think it was true, and he was sure that its time was past.

Sigmund Freud also had a healthy respect for what Christianity had done. In a brilliant lecture outlining a scientific world view, he pays respect to "religion", and he has Christianity in mind: "religion is an immense power which has the strongest emotions of human beings at its service.'' Freud says that Christianity undertakes to give human beings information about the origin and coming into being of the universe, it assures them its protection and ultimate happiness in the ups and downs of life, and it directs their thoughts and actions by precepts which it lays down with its whole authority. If it were true, Christianity would be a boon to humanity. But alas it is an illusion and has no adequate substitute. Freud bravely accepts science, but confesses that it cannot do what religion claims to do. Religion is for him the rival of science. His own contributions went a long way to providing an alternative way of life if Christianity is no longer alive. Like Karl Marx he would put it into an honourable museum, with a few horror stories to show what harm it had done during the centuries of its dominance.

Karl Marx was writing in the middle of the nineteenth century, and Freud was limited to a Darwinian view of science. Both view Christianity in a way quite different from how most believers would understand it today. Science has successfully challenged the claims of Christianity to know how the world began: Genesis is literature, not science. Freud's own psychology has changed our view of what the Church can lay down with authority about thoughts and action. We are living in a different world, but one which is strongly influenced by the thought of Marx and Freud. Neither can be ignored. And both agree that Christianity has had its day.

The steady movement of the population of Europe away from the churches seems to confirm their view. Of course there are exceptions – the Church has proved powerful in its support of ''Soladarity'' in Poland, and a strong Marxist government has not convinced the people that Marx was right about religion. Charismatic churches have mushroomed and grown in Europe and America, giving a new lease of life to churches of all denominations; Billy Graham has filled huge halls and football grounds with people who want to know whether Christianity can make sense of their life. But behind these exceptions, the steady decline of the Church goes on. Are we watching a once vital organism in its death throes? Has humanity grown out of its need for a religion?

Is Christianity True?

Part of the answer to that question is a straightforward piece of historical research. Christianity claims to be rooted in history. Jesus was born on a specific date, although it is not easy to work out exactly when. He lived in Galilee in the time of Augustus and Tiberius, and seems not to have travelled much outside his own country. He was a Jew and made a great impression by his teaching. It is said that he worked miracles of healing. He quarreled with his religious superiors, and by some intrigue was condemned to death as an insurrectionist. As was the custom, he was crucified. Not much of that would be disputed by any fair historian who studied the documents written twenty or thirty or forty years after his death. They are all contained within the New Testament, which was written entirely by those who believed the claims that either Jesus made or were made for him. Outside those New Testament documents there is practically no reference to him at all, which is hardly surprising, because he made little impact on the larger world until his followers began their missionary work. It was the Church that publicized Jesus of Nazareth. Few deny that he lived and died, but many question the claims made for him. The gospels, which contain most of the material about his life, were written in the light of the experience of the Church through one or two generations, and are therefore naturally suspect in detail. We cannot assume that the speeches reported by him, such as the three chapters of sayings that are collected in Matthew 5-7, usually called the Sermon on the Mount, were delivered by him in those precise words. But it is reasonable to suppose that those who knew him remember this as the kind of thing he taught. Some of the parables he told are so memorable that it is likely that they could remember them quite well. Some sayings are also in pithy form that could be remembered verbatim. In a largely oral culture, memory tends to be better than in a literary culture like our own. But the documents of the New Testament are full of interpretations, and these we must judge in the light of the kind of world in which the early Church grew. But more attention has been paid to these documents by scholars than to any other literature. Scholars have dated the letters, critically analysed the gospels, and tried to find out the core of experience upon which the ''books'' of the New Testament are based. It is an exciting search, which often brings alive the early Church, even if it doesn't always answer all our questions about what exactly Jesus said.

Most of the New Testament writers knew people who were with Jesus of Nazareth, and what they wrote was the impressions of those they knew, who were witnesses of the effect of Jesus upon those around him. They are worth listening to. We shall do that in a later chapter when we come to ''The Strange Relevance of the Bible''.

One of the principal sources used by Jesus seems to have been what we call the Old Testament. That is an incredible collection of documents covering a thousand years. It forms the basis of what Jesus and the first Christians were taught about the human condition.

Does it Matter?

In that collection of songs, hymns, poems and prayers which

we call the Book of Psalms, there is a hymn of praise which frames a very ancient poem. It expresses an almost universal feeling, and it portrays a person who has moved a little beyond the creed of a pagan to discover a human quality in God. The common experience is that of looking up into the heavens on a starry night, particularly when we are away from those cities and towns that shut out the stars and numb the imagination. The Hebrew poet was, no doubt, a nomad, moving from oasis to oasis, settling only occasionally for any length of time, attracted by the city, but knowing its seductive power. The stars were his common sight. The dark night of the desert is lit by the stars, and he could so easily take them for granted. Something more than ordinary stirred his mind and his sense of beauty and we can all understand

> When I consider the heavens, the work of your fingers,
> the moon and the stars, which you have set in place,
> what is man that you are mindful of him,
> the son of man that you care for him?

Today we have more cause to wonder at the immensity of the heavens. We know the extent of the universe, or rather its limitless expanses that are gradually revealed to our developing telescopes. The mathematical beauty of the heavens is also much better known to us today. The more we know about astronomy, the more wonderful the heavens become in our eyes.

Our increasing knowledge leads us to a proper sense of pride in human achievement. When a man first set foot on the moon, we talked of it as a giant step forward for mankind, and it was. But together with this justifiable pride comes a recognition of our littleness and our mortality. We uncover the mysteries of nature, but we do not produce them. We control the forces of nature, but we are observers and aware that we cannot, except on a very small scale, reproduce them. We unleash the power of the nucleus, but we are fearful that this power may move destructively out of our control. So there is pride and justifiable pride, but also a humility and a wonder before the beauty and order of the universe. The physical constants, such as the force of gravity, that we have discovered in nature are so finely balanced that if they were minutely larger or minutely smaller, we should not be there at all. A new humility has come into our science which makes us wonder at times whether its complex structure is reality at all, or perhaps a model which reflects the limitations of our own mind rather than describes the universe as it really is. But then, some dark night, we look up into the beauty of the heavens and consider. Its magnitude and its perfection leave us in wonder, and if behind all that is something or someone, what can he or it or she have to do with us? "What is man that *you* are mindful of him?"

The Human Condition

There are many religions and they probably all have some truth in them. Every culture begins with a problem which has to be solved in one way or another. It is the fragile nature of the human being before the mighty forces of nature. Even the animal kingdom threatens mankind by its strength. The psychologist Alfred Adler said that man had to develop a brain in order to survive! But man has always known that somewhere, if he could only tap it, there is a reservoir of power to sustain him. Few cultures have survived without a god. Even the communist ideology, which denies God, has to invent a substitute for God. At the Ecumenical European Assembly in Basel (1989), Christians and Communists from the Soviet Union discussed publicly their differences. One Communist leader said, "You believe in God, we believe in nature; you call yourselves children of God, we are children of nature". Then someone asked, "What is the difference between God and nature?" The speaker with a smile said, "Ask me a simpler question".

Some have seen the enormous power of nature or God and tried to discover how to get it on their side. Hinduism has recognized the great variety within the unity of what we call nature or the divine, and, like the Greeks, given special areas of influence to certain gods. The Roman Catholic does much the same with the saints – St Anthony will find a lost key for you. But in serious thought, even the Hindu will recognize the almighty power of One God – call him Brahma, Siva or Vishnu; make your sacrifices to lesser gods, but acknowledge superiority. The Muslim fiercely acknowledges only one God, and says so in defiance of all ready to hear, five times a day!

The Psalmist who framed that ancient poem in a psalm of praise recognized the God who had cared for and preserved his people, and upon whom he depended for protection from his enemies. The Christian acknowledges that same God, and sings Psalm 8 as to the God and Father of the Lord Jesus Christ.

Now in all these religions, there is a primitive phase in which the believer tries to please God, humour him if you like, so that God will be well disposed towards him. Sacrifices, gifts, good deeds, obedience to some revealed law, this will keep God on your side. But when the primitive stage is past, there is a need for true contact with the divine. Christians call it prayer, as do many other religions. But if prayer is to be more than crying to the heavens, there needs to be a line of communication. And that must come from God's side. The Jew traces his history back to a covenant between God and Abraham, and to a Law revealed to Moses which spelt out the terms of the covenant. The Muslim traces his communication back to the Prophet, to whom was revealed the Koran, whose every syllable is from God. The Koran is much more exact and more authoritative than the Bible is, either to Jew or Christian. It cannot be questioned, only explained and obeyed. The Christian finds his line of communication with God in a man, as historical as the Prophet (Mohamet), who lived in Palestine during the Roman Occupation in the first century. That man was God's initiative, showing how a human life could be lived, teaching, dying and, believers say, working miracles of healing, confronting evil wherever it was to be found in life and in death, and rising from the dead.

The heart of his teaching was that God loved the world and wanted to rescue it from the consequences of its own foolishness. More, this God whom he called Father and asked us to do also, would renew all nature and use humankind to accomplish this. He wanted the human race to inhabit the earth and to care for it, to enable it to be fruitful and multiply, and to overcome those forces that harmed it. The man Jesus taught that God wanted humans as his children. He would make them "a little lower than God" as the ancient poet said:

You made him a little lower than God
and crowned him with glory and honour.
You made him ruler over the works of your hands,
you put everything under his feet.

There is no religion which gives so high a place to man in creation as the Judaeo-Christian religion does. But both emphasize equally the wickedness and cruelty of man: "The heart of man is desperately wicked."

This tension, which we all feel, must be held. If we allow either tendency to predominate something goes out of our humanity. The one who wishes to be like God, and thinks himself or herself by nature a god, can become like Hitler. In fact, Nazism exploited this tendency in man by playing upon it in mass rallies, persuading young Germans that they were meant to rule the earth like young gods. On the other hand, if all we can recognize is the wickedness of man we destroy the vision of children of God which we are destined to become.

The Christian God

What is peculiar to the Christian religion is the belief that this God, who is behind all created things, who is the Creator and Sustainer of the universe, trusts himself to humans like us. He seeks our co-operation in his work of restoring creation to its freedom. All religions go to God in their need; our God comes to us in his need and asks our help.

There is a poem by Dietrich Bonhoeffer, a German theologian who was put to death for his opposition to Hitler, which perfectly describes this difference:

Men go to God when they are sore bestead,
Pray to him for succour, for his peace, for his bread,
For mercy for them sick, sinning or dead;
All men do so, Christian and unbelieving.

That is the common experience of men seeking help from God. We all understand it. In real trouble, many will cry, "God help us!" That does not mean a belief in God, but it does mean that the common experience of mankind is to cry for help beyond human aid. The life of Jesus, which Christians believe to be a revelation of what God is like, includes many occasions when he depended upon others. As a baby he is dependent upon a young girl who is his mother, and defended by a strong man, Joseph, who is not his father. He allows himself to be arrested and crucified. He trusts his disciples and on one occasion clearly appeals to them for help in his direst need. In the Garden of Gethsemane, he needs time to pray before the soldiers arrive to arrest him. He asks his disciples to wait and watch so that he can be warned. They fail him and he laments, "Could you not watch one little hour with me!"

Bonhoeffer, in the second stanza of that poem, catches that quality in God:

> Men go to God when he is sore bestead,
> Find him poor and scorned, without shelter or bread,
> Whelmed under weight of the wicked, the weak, the
>   dead;
> Christians stand by God in his hour of grieving.

There is a distinction there between believers and unbelievers, Christian and pagan, but it does not extend to God's help. God's care is extended to "the righteous and the unrighteous". Whether we believe in him or not, we are all potentially his children. Hence Bonhoeffer concludes the poem with:

> God goes to every man when sore bestead,
> Feeds body and spirit with his bread;
> For Christians, pagans alike he hangs dead
> And both alike forgiving.

That was the experience of those who knew the man Jesus, and he said that God is like that. One of his followers described him as saying to his disciples before he left them, "He who has seen me has seen the Father". So Christians believe that they know quite a lot about God through their study of Jesus of Nazareth.

The questions then that remain are:

How does all this work out in practice? How do you live Christianity? What do we know about Jesus of Nazareth? Are his claims to be trusted? What guidance do we have in our Christian way of life? Is the Bible of use today in giving us such guidance?

And what is our experience of Jesus Christ? Who is he for us today?

I shall have to write from my own experience, because these are personal questions, not theoretical theology. Not all Christians agree about the answers to these questions, but there is enough common ground for us to say, this is what we mean by "living Christianity".

Chapter One

A CHRISTIAN LIFE STYLE

It is, after all, the life you live that counts. On one of my visits to Bangladesh, when I was doing some educational work for the government, I was given a driver who could take me to wherever I had to go or whoever I had to meet. In that heat in Dacca it was so much better than trying to find my own way about. So I would say when and where I wanted to go, and the driver would be summoned to take me. One day I said, "Could he come at five?" The reply should not have surprised me, but it did: "Oh no ! He will be saying his prayers. A little later perhaps." There was no fuss or bother about it, no pious talk. Everybody knew his life style as a faithful Muslim. Prayer was the pattern of his day. If I had been with him during Ramadan, I would have dismissed him immediately after sunset or earlier, to allow him to get food from which he had abstained all day. All that is part of a Muslim life style.

What is a Christian life style? It usually has a pattern too, but nothing like so rigid as the Muslim. The Christian goes to church, and there the confusion begins! It depends upon which church. He may go just once on Sunday – or be involved in all kinds of activities during the week as well. His or her life style will be influenced by the people in that church. They may be a group which disapproves of alcohol, as the Muslims also do. That will mean a certain pressure not to drink in pubs. There will be certain accepted standards of sexual behaviour, and the use of language. There is almost sure to be an assumption that he will keep on the right side of the law. A church group very often has definite ideas about how a Christian should behave, but not always. They may and should let an individual Christian develop his or her own life in accordance with growing experience and beliefs. There should be a freedom about it. When I first joined a church, I soon discovered that a whole mythology of Christian behaviour had grown up, and with it a pattern which could have filled my week. I was expected to pray and read the Bible. But when I had read the Bible I was surprised. These religious people had said, "Read the Bible every day!"; I did.

Balancing the Pressures

The Bible was my surprise because I found it was hostile to religion. I began to wonder why those older Christians had advised me to read it. Had *they* read it? Most of the Old Testament prophets, whom I early warmed to, seemed to say that religion was not very important. What mattered was the kind of life you lived every day. Of course, they were angry when the Israelites worshipped other gods, but that was another religion they were against. As for the "true" religion, they portrayed God as sick of their burnt offerings and their solemn assemblies. One even stood at the door of their temple and ridiculed their religion. God was not impressed by people who said in pious tones, "The Temple of the Lord", just as Jesus seemed little impressed by those who called him "Lord, Lord" and claimed to do all kinds of miracles in his name. There was a very distinct pressure coming from the Bible which didn't fit in with the pattern of life lived in church circles.

The Bible awakened something in me and resonated ideas that were part of my inner self. I knew that I was partly in charge of my own life and that people could influence me. Religion, however, seemed to go further than that. It laid down guidelines which I must follow. There were rules in this religious community, and I soon discovered that the word "religion" means restraining with bonds. And this I did not like. One of the surprises was to discover how little the Bible has to say about "religion". The word is not used in the Old Testament at all, and in the New it is often with disapproval or in need of correction. It is either the Jews' religion or it is just a description of a man's way of life which, if it is not compassionate, is rebuked. But there is one reference which clearly shows how different these Christians are from just religious people. It is in the Letter of James:

> If any one thinks he is *religious*, and does not bridle his tongue but deceives his heart, this man's *religion* is vain. Religion that is pure and undefiled before God the Father is this: to visit orphans and widows in their affliction, and to keep oneself unstained from the world.

The first part of that definition is all right, but the second worried me. Paul said something similar in his long letter to the Romans, "Don't be conformed to this world", or as J.B. Phillips translated it most helpfully, "Don't let the world around you squeeze you into its mould". I first had to recognize that this meant quite a lot more than "Don't go to dance halls or pubs or cinemas". It meant resisting those pressures that distorted you. That was my first glimmer of the truth that being a follower of Christ did not mean being like all the others – even like the other "Christians" – but it meant being yourself.

The more I read the gospels, and particularly when I saw that you have to make allowance for the long passage of time between the actual teaching of Jesus and writing it down, the more I realized that Jesus was not very religious. One evangelist says that he went to synagogue, "as his custom was", but every time he is described as going to synagogue, he gets into trouble, either for what he does or what he says. He really does ride rough shod over their views of the sacredness of the Sabbath, and his follower Paul threw out circumcision, the most religious mark of any Jew. At least he left me feeling that I could challenge the demands of religion in the name of common sense and humanity. Where now is the direction for a life style? Not from the church. Those fellow believers may help me, but they must not be allowed to distort me. The Bible too had to be read with care, because it concerned a society very different from the one I was living in. It could not be taken literally, although it should be read seriously. I found it of enormous help in balancing the pressures. It seemed to concentrate on the way I related to other people.

The only commandment Jesus gave was "to love one another", and to the dismay of the religious, he summarized all the laws of religion in two precepts: **Love God** and **love your neighbour as yourself**. Perhaps there are three there. In fact all three are one. You cannot love God, neighbour or self in isolation. Try it and you soon find out how odd it is. Jesus has a lot to say about that. So does John. It permeates the New Testament. Christianity isn't really a religion at all; it's a way of life. And it is a way of learning how to love. That inner self which is violated by the injustice done to a fellow being, that problem which society puts to you when it is unprofitable to care for a victim of the rat race, the call for help at an inconvenient moment, the temptation not to notice. There are a hundred examples we can all produce of the conflicts of interest. Test them by the threefold love. That seemed to me the best way to balance the pressures.

Of course, some of these pressures are destructive drives – greed, lust, ambition, anger, etc. They too must face the test, not of rules, but of the threefold love. We shall have to look at these in the next chapter on "The principal conflicts", but let us recognize at once that balancing the pressures upon us is neither a simple matter of deciding what is right and what is wrong, nor arranging pretty patterns. It can be a bloody struggle.

Towards a Life Style

Someone who is committed to Christ is called a Christian, but that is not what these followers of Jesus Christ called themselves. The word "Christian" only occurs three times in the New Testament, and always with reference to what others called believers in Christ. They first got that nickname some years after the Church had been founded. One of the earliest leaders of the company of believers came to Antioch with a controversial convert who had been waiting a long time. Over the space of about a year they met and taught a large number of people. Luke, who wrote up that story, comments: "and in Antioch the disciples were for the first time called Christians" (Acts 11:26). Years later when that controversial convert had become one of the most vigorous missionaries and changed his name to Paul, he was on trial before King Agrippa, who interrupted his defence, saying: "In a short time you think to make me a Christian?" Paul does not use the word in reply, but simply wishes that all the court might be "such as I am except for these chains".

And the only other reference to "Christians" is in a letter from Peter to some followers of Jesus Christ who are facing persecution. He advises them to make sure that they are not accused of criminal offences, for which they should like all others be punished, but only accused of being "Christians". If they call you that and punish you for it, then be glad: "yet if one suffers as a Christian, let him not be ashamed, but under that name let him glorify God''. The first believers thought of themselves as disciples, followers of the Way, worshippers of God the Father of the Lord Jesus Christ, or even as ''saints''. That last title meant only those separated for God's service. We have accepted the name Christian now, but would rather be without labels. They come thick and fast, but always from others – Baptist, Methodist, Anglican, are all nicknames.

A life style for one who believes in God and follows the way of Jesus Christ begins in our humanity, not in any particular group with a label.

So begin, with gratitude to those scientists who have explored the mind and helped us to understand ourselves better. We know that our bodies have animal ancestry. The whole God-infested process of Evolution has produced the human species; but our body is not us. We use it as an instrument, finely interwoven with our mind and spirit. All are inter-dependent, with no special place for a soul or a spirit to slip in and out. We are one. Each person is a miracle of construction. As humans we have a greater responsibility than the animals have – it is the nature of beasts to be beastly, but of humans to be humane. The animal nature follows its own laws; we humans have control to a certain extent. We have, however, learnt from Sigmund Freud and others that there is a vast unexplored territory of our mind which we call the unconscious. There lie the unresolved problems of our infancy, the repressions of facts about ourselves that we could not face. There too lie great creative powers and memories of our race. It comes into our consciousness in dreams, in creative exercises and at crucial moments in our lives. Thus while we may live by reason, carefully noting what is required of us and in all things doing our duty, there are times of sweeping passions that seem out of our control. We are rational creatures, but there are times when "the good we would do that we do not", or even more truthfully, "that which we would not that we do". We may fix the parameters of our life style, based upon our understanding of what is required of us, but it is not reason alone that rules our lives. Jesus did not say, "Be reasonable with your neighbour". Reason has its place, but love is the determining factor for our life style.

What is Love?

Animals can mate; humans can also love. There are so many definitions and varied expressions. Love has given us our greatest poetry. Of all the philosophers, Nietzsche has more than anyone else caught the mystery of this illusive relationship between two people: "Love is to protect the beloved from shame." There can be no human so depraved that he or she has never loved and been loved. When humans are isolated and lonely they will bestow that relationship upon a cat or a dog, thinking to find some equivalent to human love in the response of an animal. They will often find it, because we have domesticated animals and they have learnt our ways. But basically, love is a relationship between persons. It overrides all considerations of profit, and it is destroyed when used to exploit the other. Love gives and receives with joy. It does not calculate and it has an extraordinary power of endurance. "Love never fails", Paul writes, and we know in our hearts that this is true, although the evidence often points the other way.

Love will always include some form of sexual attraction. This can be seen in the love of the saints for God. St Teresa of Avila is rightly portrayed by the artists as in an ecstasy which does not differ greatly from the ecstasy of a satisfied sexual relationship. This is not to diminish the spirituality of her devotion to God, it is to recognize that her love for God is a human love. But while love contains a sexual expression it is not exhausted by that, because we are more than animals. That something more is our humanity, and we find it in the relationship of two whole persons to each other. Those who were offended by the novel and even more by the film, *The Last Temptation*, were unable to recognize a sexual element in the love of Jesus. Without it he would not have been fully human, and what Christians call the Incarnation would have been only partial. The film rather than the book erred by concentrating upon the physical expression of this sexual element in the fantasy which offended so many. It failed to demonstrate the extraodinary extent to which Jesus sublimated his sexual desires. Jesus showed the way to deal with love that cannot find its expression in a sexual relationship without destroying at least one of the participants in it. Love is more than sex, and the act of ''sublimation'' is the discovery of the human potential. The love poem, the creative exercise in art or music, the perfecting of a life style, the search for holiness, all these and more can emerge from a sublimated love.

If there is any truth in what some scholars have called a homosexual relationship between Jesus and his disciples, then it is powerfully sublimated in the achievement of these disciples after his resurrection. If Mary Magdalene was in love with Jesus it is hardly surprising, and the scene in the garden after his death depicts a woman in despair at the death of her loved one. The words of Jesus to her, ''Do not touch me'', is a gentle sublimation of her love. She discovered her true love for him in announcing the triumph of the beloved in his risen state. A sublimated love is the giving of the whole person in the loving relationship in which the body is a transitory instrument. We have more to give than that.

How Can We Love God?

The New Testament is insistent that we love God, because he first loved us. But how do we know that God loves us? There is about as much evidence as for the lover who asks, "How do I know that he [or she] loves me?" There are first of all his actions. The evidence is ambiguous, but the world is very beautiful and it seems to be cared for beyond our industry. This is the pagan's creed, but it cannot be discounted.

There are those too who tell of God's care in their distress, even of healing wrought by prayer. There are those who can show how what they have done they could not have done in their own strength. Even nationally and among the nations, men and women have done terrible things, but some hand has restrained them from final destruction. It is hard to believe in a good and caring God after the appalling atrocities of the concentration camps, but something held back the victorious advances of the Nazi hordes. We have many horrid things in our world, but Wordsworth is not the only poet who has seen hope in the eyes of a child. Intellectually, we may not agree with the poet that we come from God and once knew his love far better than we do now, but few can resist those lines which find echoes in our memory:

> Our birth is but a sleep and a forgetting:
> The Soul that rises with us, our life's Star,
> Hath had elsewhere its setting,
> and cometh from afar:
> Not in entire forgetfulness,
> And not in utter nakedness,
> But trailing clouds of glory do we come
> From God, who is our home:
> Heaven lies about us in our infancy!

Wordsworth called that poem, *Intimations of Immortality from Recollections of Early Childhood.*

God's Chosen Race

The persistent faith of the Jewish people, which has kept them during terrible centuries of persecution and brought them to become a people once again after centuries of exile, is based upon the firm conviction that long ago God brought them up out of Egypt. The saga which is told in the Old Testament is about the birth of a people and the formation of a nation by a loving God. He worked through men and women, like Moses, but he cared. The stories are fierce at times, and God is portrayed as angry and even vengeful, but behind that picture there is a God who loves and who calls forth love in response. A people has been preserved throughout history by this firm conviction, repeated in the best known creed of the Jewish religion, nailed on every doorpost of the faithful Jewish family – the *Shema*:

> Hear, O Israel, The Lord our God is one Lord; and
> you shall love the Lord your God with all your
> heart, and with all your soul, and with all your
> might.

Because of that love, they believed that God had laid upon them certain laws by which they should live, to preserve them because he loved them and had a destiny for them. They saw that everything was in the hands of their God, and when dreadful things happened to them which almost extinguished them as a race, they did not give up their belief in a God who loved them, but saw God's correction in it. There are many stories of Jewish faithfulness in times of disaster. One from modern times is as telling as any I know.

It was during the awful experience of Auschwitz. A company of Jews put God on trial for what he was allowing to happen to his people in Nazi Germany. They found him guilty and then the Rabbi said, "It is time for evening prayers". And they assembled to pray to their God! You cannot dismiss a history like that of the Jews. But does it not tell only of God's love for some people and in particular the Jews? Already among the Prophets who are recorded in the Old Testament there is a strong emphasis on Israel's destiny as for the whole world. Abraham was promised that in him "all the nations of the earth will be blessed". But the universal love of God is most clearly shown in a poem by an unknown prophet whose songs are included in the Book of Isaiah.

It was around 500 BC, when the Jews had lost their city, and their beloved temple had gone up in flames. The leaders of the people were deported to Babylon and were at the mercy of their conquerors. There was a natural depression among the Jews, who felt that God had given them up. Prophets had warned that their way of life and their greed would lead to this, but that didn't make it easier to bear. God no longer loved them. The complaint was that he had taken so much trouble throughout history – rescuing them from Egypt, guiding them through the wilderness for a generation, preparing them to settle in the Promised Land, and giving them a destiny. All this seems to have been in vain. What was God up to? In the midst of this depression, a poet arose who probably sang his poems.

Verdi, in his opera *Nabucco*, perfectly depicts this unnamed singer when in one scene he shows the Jews as slaves on the way to Babylon. They are utterly exhausted and lie as dead people on the stage. The music reflects their despair. Then one voice rises above the music and the singer stands up. His song brings them slowly to their feet, until they all stand upright singing the song as a song of triumph. The guards look uneasy. They no longer have a docile people, but a people who believe in themselves and in their

God. Outwardly, nothing has changed in their desperate situation, but they have changed. God loves them. One of the four songs which are included in the Book of Isaiah tells of the complaint that God has deserted them, and also of the discovery of their destiny. It is in the form of question (or rather complaint) and answer. The people complain that God has prepared them for greatness and given them slavery. The reply from the Lord is that he has prepared them for greatness, but not the kind they expect:

> It is too light a thing that you should be my servant to raise up the tribes of Jacob and to restore the preserved of Israel;
> I will give you as a light to the nations, that my salvation may reach to the ends of the earth.

At the heart of the Jews' faith in God is that he chooses them specially for a task which will eventually show his love for all mankind.

"God so loved the world"

Jesus was a Jew and so were all his disciples. The most outstanding exponent of his life and teaching who joined the disciples later came from the very strictest group of Jews. The community that formed around a belief that God had specially chosen Jesus of Nazareth and raised him from the dead was a Jewish community. It came to believe that God had taken the initiative in sending this man Jesus to fulfil all that the Jewish community had longed for and understood of God's love. Here in this man was to be that light for the nations, through him God's salvation would reach the ends of the earth.

A great deal of doctrine was added to that later, but in its infant freshness this belief in Jesus as the servant of God, the Christ or Messiah sent by God, the one who could show us what God was like and the pattern for those who would love God, appeals still.

If we are to find a life style which incorporates love of God, love of self and love of neighbour, we must find our model in the life, death and resurrection of Jesus. There is more to be said about the grace needed for such an heroic effort, but it begins in this simple "imitation of Christ". It was for that reason that at least four writers, after all the arguments and controversies, after the quarrels with their fellow Jews, decided to write down as much as they could discover of the life of Jesus, his teaching and the way he died, leading to their central belief that God raised him from the dead. These four writers gave us the four gospels with which our New Testament rightly opens.

Jesus not only taught his disciples to love God, he showed them that God was lovable, and bade them address him as "Father" in the most intimate form that might almost be translated as "Daddy". He did not argue that God loved them, he showed the nature of the love of God who longed to have all humans as his children. He not only taught his disciples to love themselves, he showed them that they had worth. He not only taught that they should love their neighbours, he loved them – the despised collaborators with the Roman tax system, the women of the street and one taken in adultery. He showed that love did not depend upon being righteous, but upon the innate worth of a human being made in the image of God, despite all its disfigurement. He discerned God in every person, and to those who loved him he said, look closely at the face of that beggar and you will see that it is my face. He loved those who tormented him, and of those who crucified him he said, "Father, forgive them, for they know not what they do".

These are the rudiments of a life style. They depend upon the acceptance of the fact that God loves us and gives us worth. With that dignity, beloved children of God, how can we fail to love our neighbours? His teaching even shows us what is meant by "neighbour". The answer is given in the parable of the Good Samaritan. Our neighbour is the one we encounter in his or her need. The help we give depends upon his or her need, not upon whether such a one deserves help. The followers of Jesus are those who help the undeserving poor also.

In an introduction to a little book, *Making Men Whole*, J.B Phillips, the popular translator of the New Testament (and *Four Prophets* from the Old), lists five guidelines for living Christianity in this world. When I first read them in 1952, I responded at once because of their basic and self-evident truth, attested by the experience of many:

1. The world remains primarily God's responsibility. Our task is to find out our part in his plan.

2. Think in terms of the little things in life. Love has to be seen incarnate in a human being and therefore let us "base our methods on what we see Christ do".

3. It is not enough to concern ourselves with Christian ethics. The experience with Christ is seen rather as an "invasion of our lives by the Spirit of God".

4. The purpose of God in dealing with humanity seems to be to bring us together. I must ask, "Am I co-operating or not?"

5. Human life is not limited to "the cradle to the grave". It has to be lived in the setting of eternity. God calls us to be beings aware of the eternal dimensions of our lives. "We must recover the wonder and glory of the calling wherewith we are called."

Living in this World.

There are so many high-sounding phrases in Christian literature that there is a danger of opting out of this world and preferring the other-worldly way of life. That can be lived among an isolated community – a monastery or temporarily in a religious conference – and it can even be the life one lives as a member of a church – a part life. The danger is in splitting: one life lived in the church with its own vocabulary and statements of truth and doctrine. That life can be stimulated by disagreeing with another group, who believe a little differently. Then there is much heat, if little light, produced, as you demonstrate how right your group is and how wrong the other is. But unless you live in isolation, there must be another life lived at work and at home. Unless you are to be schizophrenic, these two must be related. Endless discussions in church will not do it, even if you do discuss how the Christian faith can be applied. It has to be lived, not discussed. One could imagine a church where its members lived according to a life style and met every week to discuss in a practical way where they had failed. Mutual help and correction could be a great help in living real life, which is not in the church, but in the world.

Kierkegaard, a Danish philosopher who lived last century and was always prodding his church, wrote an allegory of a church which lived two separated lives. He called it, in his *Journals*, "The Domestic Goose – a stirring meditation".

"Imagine that geese could talk", he opens, and deduces that they would arrange their own church services. Every Sunday, they would meet together and a gander would preach! He describes their worship and the content of the preaching which is "the exalted destiny of geese". This consists of using their wings and flying away to distant countries. Of course, this is in the realm of the "other-worldly" and they have no such ambitions during the week.

Instead they grow plump and tender and are eaten at Christmas! The sermon inspired them on Sunday, but on Monday, "they would tell one another of the fate of the goose who wanted to take her high destiny seriously, with the help of the wings the Creator had given her". They spoke of the horrors she had to endure. Then they noticed some of the younger geese looking ill and thin and wisely commented, "You see what comes of being serious about wanting to fly. It is because they are always thinking of flying, that they get thin and do not thrive, and do not have God's grace as we do. That is why we get plump and fat and tender, for it is by God's grace that one gets plump and fat and tender." On the next Sunday they went back to church and heard the same sermon of "the exalted destiny of geese" and the far countries to which they would fly.

It is a caricature, of course, but it is near enough to the bone for eager worshippers to recognize the dangers.

What then should we do if the values of the Church are so different from those of the world around us? Certainly separation is no answer. It leads to hypocrisy – saying one thing and doing another, inspiring one another with high thoughts, but knowing they are not practical in the real world.

Look at those five guidelines again (see p.14). The first and the last are really the framework which determine our attitude. We may not like many things that go on in the world. If God is primarily responsible then he must be at work somewhere opposing these false values. If our lives are set in eternity then we are not going to get frantic about not having enough time. The world was there before we came and will be there, we hope, after we have gone. During our lifetime, we do not have to succeed or complete a task. We need to discover our part in God's warfare against evil. Christians talk much about the kingdom of God and pray in their most common prayer, "Thy kingdom come!" They therefore want God's rule to predominate, not their political party, nor their particular solution to the problems. There should be a relaxed attitude if we have eternity as our measure and if God is primarily responsible, so long as we have tried to find our place in God's plan. That is the opposite of expecting God to be on our side.

Then there is that second guideline which cuts us down to size. It is so much easier to talk about nuclear disarmament, unemployment, homelessness, the violation of nature, than to act in all these areas of concern. The words are needed because we have a political responsibility as citizens, but all have that, believer and non-believer alike. As Christians, we have to conquer the hatred in our hearts, which is of the same nature as that which would press the button to destroy one's threatening enemy. We have to care for the unemployed whom we know, and give them hope and purpose in daily life. Perhaps we have to take the homeless into our homes, or at least not pass by that thin young man sitting silently with a card before him reading "Hungry and Homeless". We need to mend our own life style and care for the creation by the way we use resources. It is not statistics which will destroy the life-giving beauty of this planet, but people.

A Christian life style is a life lived in this world and not only in church.

Let me end this chapter with Kierkegaard again, because he had to speak clearly to a generation of Christians who were content to separate their lives into church and world. A Christian life style for them had to do with religious things, not secular. He describes a "Knight of Faith", i.e. one who illustrates in his life the high spiritual qualities of his faith, the champion of the Christian way of life. His description is a shock:

"Good God! Is that really him? He looks like an Inspector of Taxes!"

But it really is him. Kierkegaard goes on to describe how he tries to find out his secret. This bourgeois man - yet he is a "knight of faith". Draw closer and watch every movement,

> to see whether he shows any sign of the least telegraphic communication with the infinite, a glance, a look, a gesture, an air of melancholy, a smile to betray the contrast of infinity and the finite. But no! I examine him from head to foot, hoping to discover a chink through which the infinite can peer. But no! He is completely solid.

Kierkegaard goes on to describe a perfectly ordinary person who enjoys life and eats well. He seems fully at home in the world. What happens when he goes to church on Sunday, surely then we shall see some heavenly trace, but no!

> No heavenly glance, no sign of incommensurability betrays him; and without knowing him it would be impossible to distinguish him from the rest of the congregation, for his healthy bellowing of the psalms proves only that he has a good pair of lungs.

And when he takes his Sunday afternoon walk his step has no special lightness in it.

> He is not a poet . . . When he comes home he walks as sturdily as a postman.

The secret is discovered, in a way typical of Kierkegaard, in his dancing. It is the slight falter as he lands after a leap. The knight of faith is one for whom the earth is seen rather differently. It is in fact J.B. Phillips's fifth guideline: Human life has an eternal dimension and there is a wonder and glory in our calling.

The Christian Motivation

The behaviour of a Christian may not look very different from that of anyone else, but its motivation could be different and its continuance reliable.

Take the three issues which in recent years have become so important for the churches and for the world: peace, justice and the integrity of creation.

Peace is sought for its own sake, because this is how God wishes his children to live together, without hatred or despising one another. Only thus can he bring them together and achieve his purpose for them. Unless peace is sought in that way and for that reason the roots of conflict will remain and grow like weeds that have been cut down.

Justice is sought because it is the way in which God deals with us. And that includes forgiveness. Justice without mercy is not the justice we learn from the way God deals with us. Only thus can we avoid giving a more just dealing to the powerful than we do to the powerless. And once that distinction is admitted, we know that the division will deepen and there will be no voice for the powerless. The strong will be deemed right because they are strong.

The integrity of creation is seen as our responsibility under God for all created things, to care for and not to exploit. Nature is not ours, it is our workshop, wherein we discover our potential and wherein nature itself is set free. The purpose of God is to fulfil his creation and he does this by the interdependence of humanity and nature. The integrity of creation is our integrity. If our only concern for nature is that it should continue to supply resources for our existence we shall find ways of extracting what we need without due regard to the planet on which we live. We shall become like parasites on the living body of nature.

Chapter Two

CONFLICTING IDEAS

A Christian life style should give a sense of freedom – from petty rules and regulations, from "the burden of the Law". But that does not mean an irresponsible life. In fact, a responsible life lived in freedom is a great deal more difficult and makes much greater demands than a life hedged about by a precise code of conduct. It is said that at the time of the liberation of the slaves in North America, several slaves returned to their former masters and asked to be taken back. They found the demands of an open society more than they could cope with. The account of the liberation of the Hebrew slaves in Egypt, told in the Book of Exodus, is full of complaints that they were better off in slavery. There are, of course, some basic guidelines. There are also self-evident rights and wrongs, but it is important not to make these too absolute. The way we use some of the letters that Paul wrote to the churches should warn us against this. He is really only giving advice to young churches on how to behave in their particular circumstances. We misuse his texts if we insist that women should wear hats in church or that wives should be subject to their husbands. Even "children, obey your parents" is not absolute law! We are called to freedom and warned not to use our freedom to create moral chaos.

"God's Law and God's Love"
Norman Anderson, in a book of this title (Collins, 1980) has a telling example from the gospels which shows how Jesus adhered to the Law as a good Jew, but rejected those

traditions which denied the principle behind the Law. It is
from Mark 7 and Matthew 15, where Jesus was criticized by
the Pharisees because his disciples came in from the market
place and started eating without ceremoniously washing
their hands:

> But he was wholly unmoved and immediately went
> over to the offensive by telling them that they on their
> part, had completely nullified and set aside the
> commandment of God in the Decalogue (Ten
> Commandments) itself, that a man should honour his
> father and mother, by the expedient of decreeing that,
> should he say his goods were vowed or dedicated to the
> Temple (''Corban''), he was forthwith legally
> forbidden to use them for the use of his parents' needs.
> Then, for good measure, he took the opportunity to
> explain to his disciples, that a man is made spiritually
> unclean not by the omission of some outward or
> ceremonial requirement, but by the evil thoughts and
> deeds which well up from his inner being.

Jesus consistently teaches like this. In the Sermon on the
Mount he takes those Ten Commandments, which to this
day have a kind of authority which is difficult to resist, and
explores their true meaning in the concrete situations of daily
life. In every case, he directs them towards love rather than
law.

Thou shalt not kill. Although that command is generally
accepted, and most civilized countries maintain it by law,
there are always qualifications. Of course, it means ''do no
murder'', we usually say, and proceed to exclude killing in
wartime (''lawful killing''), killing by neglect, killing
accidentally as in car crashes, euthanasia, abortion, and
even use that ugly word ''manslaughter'' to mitigate the

heinous crime of murder. But Jesus refers to none of these things, because he is less concerned with law courts than with human relations. He delves into the attitudes that may lead eventually to the crime of murder – anger, abuse, despising your brother. Put these attitudes right and we have no need to repeat the commandments. Such attitudes make it impossible for us to love or worship God. Jesus, as is his style, puts this into a brief and vivid parable:

> So if you are offering your gift at the altar, and there remember that your brother has something against you, leave your gift there before the altar and go; first be reconciled to your brother and then come and offer your gift.

Thou shalt not commit adultery. Although that command is generally accepted, and is maintained by law for the stability of family life, there are generally accepted qualifications. Every case must be considered on its merits. The Church of England has at last recognized that a person who has been divorced may under certain conditions be accepted for ordination. A law is questioned. A loveless marriage may lead one or other partner to discover in someone else the love which he or she longs for. Jesus does not discuss this, although he refuses to condemn the woman taken in adultery. Instead he once again directs attention away from the law to love in human relationships. It is the man's attitude to the woman, and in our society he would have said equally the attitude of the woman to the man, which is the central concern. What he calls ''looking at a woman lustfully'' is the treatment of the other person as an instrument of pleasure rather than a full person. It is isolating the physical sexual act from the love which it is intended to express which makes adultery a perversion.

What Jesus has to say about the sexual relationships of man
and woman is very sparse, but it is clear. He understands
love and does not condemn its expression. At the same time
he retains the sacredness of marriage, as the verses following
declare. This is not easy to work out in different cultural
settings. But he warns us strongly enough about turning this
into a matter of law. Human relationships are free and must
be entered into with equal dignity; there is no place for
dominance in love. Each is servant to the other.

In much the same way he deals with **oaths**. They are to be
honestly taken with open meaning, giving one's word, but
not with delphic duplicity.

The much quoted "eye for an eye" does not appeal to
Jesus. Some people seem to quote it as though it were the
basic teaching of the Bible , but even in the Old Testament it
is a restraining law to prevent feuds. When revenge is the
order of the day, then restraint is needed. A tribe which
revenges the loss of an eye with the massacre of an enemy
family is held in check by getting an exact equivalent of
injury. In Shakespeare's *Merchant of Venice* , Portia admits the
justice of the pound of flesh, but will not allow one drop of
blood! That is law used within its own limitations and
requiring mercy for its proper operation. In this conflict,
however, between law and love, Jesus puts himself on the
side of love. His audience must have been shocked by his
commentary, which seems to dismiss equal recompense
altogether: "Do not resist one who is evil." This is
illustrated by turning the other cheek, going the extra mile,
phrases that have entered into our language. Perhaps he goes
a bit far with, "Give to him who begs from you and do not
refuse him who would borrow from you". Not many
Christians take that as their way of life, but he has shattered
the claims of law. We cannot, after that, do less than Paul
advocated: "If your enemy hunger, feed him."

Telling the Truth

From our infancy, this basic ethical principle is taught to us all, Christians and Unbelievers. There are exceptional cases where lying is deliberately taught, and even more where lying is learnt by observation. Nevertheless, in most families the child is taught to tell the truth, but there are qualifications. The parents demand complete truth from the child; but do not reciprocate. The child is perhaps too young to be told the truth, without qualification. From the harmless Father Christmas legend, or stories about birth, to the explanations of death, the parent is required to fabricate. The child also learns that the truth is told completely only within the limited circle of the family. Telling the truth means something different according to the particular situation in which one stands. Do we have a right to ask or even demand truth from others? It depends upon the relationship between the people speaking. The truth which is conveyed by a statement is also different and dependent upon the relationship. Take an example which in fact Bonhoeffer gives in his prison writings:

> A teacher asks a child in front of the class whether it is true that his father often comes home drunk. It is true, but the child denies it. The teacher's question has placed him in a position for which he is not yet prepared. He feels only that what is taking place is an unjustified interference in the order of the family, and he must oppose it. What goes on in the family is not for the ears of the class in school. The family has its own secret and must preserve it. The teacher has failed to respect the reality of this institution. The child ought now to find a way of answering which would comply with both the rule of the family and the rule of the school. But he is not yet able to do this. He lacks

experience, knowledge and the ability to express himself in the right way. As a simple "no" to the teacher's question the child's answer is untrue; yet at the same time it nevertheless gives expression to the truth that the family is an institution *sui generis* and that the teacher had no right to interfere in it.

The child's answer is a lie, but it contains more truth than if he had betrayed his father's weakness before the whole class. The blame for the lie is therefore the teacher's.

That is a telling example because it shows the conflict between a simple precept which few would deny, i.e. telling the truth, and the reality of the situation. Living Christianity is to be sensitive to that conflict. The words of a statement may be correct, but deliberately intended to mislead. Then a correct statement is a lie.

The example of the boy and the teacher also reminds us that there is a proper place for concealment. Not everything has to be revealed. There are relations between people which may properly belong only to those people, and it is a misunderstanding to call the revelation of those relationships truth. We have glaring examples of this in the popular press. Some revelation of privacy is published with a great show of virtue. The people have a right to know! The conflict here is between privacy, confidentiality, trust on the one hand, and the claims of truth on the other. Carl Gustav Jung, the Swiss psychologist, in the course of his confrontation with the unconscious, said in a moment of unusual clarity, "Now you possess a key to mythology and are free to unlock all the gates of the unconscious psyche". But, he tells us that something whispered within him, "Why open all the gates?"

There are certain conditions under which a Christian has a right to tell the truth about another person, and conditions under which he or she has a duty to conceal. The obvious example is that of betrayal and at the heart of the story of the crucifixion stands Judas, who told the truth when he kissed Jesus. But not every situation is as simple. Some leading questions have to be asked if the conflict is to be resolved:

Am I entitled to speak?

Who requires this truth from me, and have they the right to my confidence?

Why do I want to speak, and is this the right place in which to reveal what I have to say?

In the context of these questions, what effect do I intend upon the object of my revelation?

It is, of course, much easier to tell the truth without bothering about all these questions. The George Washington approach of "I cannot tell a lie" is more heroic, but less sensitive to the nature of Christian morality. There is often a serious conflict here.

Time and Eternity

The agony which afflicted the believers in Corinth was that perhaps death was the end. They believed in the return of Christ to earth, but they could not see how their friends and loved ones who had meanwhile died could share in the celebrations. Their concern was not the theological one of whether the tomb was empty on Easter morning, but would the dead rise? Paul dealt with their problems in the fifteenth chapter of what is called his First Letter to the Corinthians. He reminded them of his preaching, which included as always the fact of the resurrection of Christ, and from that he deduced for them the certainty of the resurrection of the dead. This heady preaching, that life continued and enlarged after death, led many to despise the earthly life as merely an unpleasant preliminary to true life after death. And to this day there are those who say that without resurrection, life makes no sense. Now that is an illusion and presents us with another of our principal conflicts.

J.B Phillips's fifth guideline was "Human life has an eternal dimension and there is a wonder and a glory in our calling" which can direct our attention entirely beyond death to the glory that is to be. Then rightly, someone asks, "Is there a life before death?" And the answer has to be yes, a very important life, and it is that life which has an eternal dimension. Many people do not believe in eternal life, and for many of them life does make sense: loving, hating, being born, dying, working, struggling, seeking, making mistakes, beginning again, finding, taking and giving pleasure, truth, justice, goodness, beauty. You do not have to believe in eternal life to think that all this makes sense. The meaning may be limited, not easy to understand, but none the less it exists independently of faith in an eternal life. We cannot claim, "Without eternal life nothing makes sense". Although we can view our life in time as an interval in a larger span, the conflict arises if we ignore or despise the very life in time to which our faith gives an eternal significance.

How then do we balance the significance of the life we live here in time with the glory that is to be? We can find our help in unexpected places. Psychiatrists have shown that there is a familiar neurosis that comes from a conviction that an object exists which would fulfil every desire. As most psycho-analysts are not believers and have no conviction about eternal life, we may suspect their conclusions that for many people this desired object is made into God. But they are probably right. Even the Hebrew prophets like Isaiah were suspicious of people who make their own gods. Isaiah in a very satirical passage pokes fun at the idol makers, who chop down a tree and after using the wood that can be made into furniture and used for building houses, take the residue, the useless parts of the tree, burn some and make the rest into a god. His comment is "they feed on ashes". No doubt there is a failed father behind many religious impulses that desire a god that does not fail. But when the analysis proceeds deeper, and if we follow some psychoanalysts after Freud, we soon discover that "the substitute for father" will not explain it all. In fact that desire for a god who will fulfil all that we long for often perverts our idea of God. While we need to recognize this perversion of God as one who fulfils all our desires, we must not pervert the humanity of mankind. What is perverted is a distortion of something very true and very human. There is in all people a true longing for the infinite, and it is not just a desire to be made safe and to go on living for ever in eternity. It is a recognizable characteristic in "all" and we fail to understand a person, however degraded, unless we recognize this. This desire for the infinite is a basic factor of human existence, and far more the source of our greatness and our vitality than it is of our illusions and our failings. Even those who do not believe in God or eternal life can often be found with a very firm desire for a transcendent quality in their life. Few are prepared to reduce life to biology and chemistry. Love, beauty, fairness, compassion, self-sacrifice and other such qualities are common among many who do not believe.

One of our principal conflicts is the stubborn fact of the goodness and transcendent quality of the life of many a non-believer. Theologians have exhausted themselves over the ages in trying to emphasize the wonder of the transcendent, the heavenly or eternal life, at the expense of finding human life brutish and evil. Heaven becomes an escape from a wicked world. But nothing in the teaching of Jesus encourages us to think of human life, here and now, like that – and it is contrary to our experience. Life is good. So the conflict is between being "heavenly minded" without being "no earthly good". In fact, it is not necessarily a conflict; it can be a resolution.

Go back to the Sermon on the Mount. Jesus encourages his disciples not to be over-anxious about earthly things – food, clothes, the future. God can be trusted. He sums up what he has been saying with, "But seek first his kingdom and righteousness, **and all these things shall be yours as well**". When your mind is really on the heavenlies, not dreaming of possibilities, but knowing the eternal and transcendent, then anxieties vanish away and you can enjoy earthly things. The wine of heaven makes the wines of earth taste bitter!

Even in Hinduism, which tends to mortify the flesh and despise this world in favour of the spiritual beyond, there is a strain that catches this truth. The importance of the earthly as the workshop where spiritual truths are fashioned for eternity is repeatedly stressed in Rabindranath Tagore, the leading Bengali poet of this century. It is stressed also in the poems of Basava, the twelfth-century spiritual leader and statesman in South India. He compares the world to "the Maker's mint" and declares that coins minted here have currency in heaven!

All religions face the problem of relating time to eternity. Occasionally our hymns express the desire for this relationship to be fruitful. One at least rejects the idea of concentrating the mind on heaven to the extent of despising earth:

> My God, I love Thee, not because
> I hope for heaven thereby;
> Nor because they who love Thee not
> Are lost eternally.

Once God's love is manifest, as in the death of Jesus, our love is a response not an insurance policy. And that response has to be made in the world, in time in fact.

> E'en so I love Thee, and will love,
> And in Thy praise will sing,
> Because Thou art my loving God,
> And my redeeming King.

Time and eternity are met in that response.

Sexuality

The Church has singularly failed over the centuries to deal adequately with one of the commonest and most intimate relationships between people – the sexual relationship. The extreme position of the Roman Catholic Church has been intensified by two of the most recent Popes: Pope Paul VI went to Latin America, where large families imposed grinding poverty upon so many faithful Catholics, and reaffirmed the traditional condemnation of contraception. The present Pope John Paul II is even more fiercely determined to maintain traditional teaching. Neither Pope has been much heeded among large sections of the Catholic population. But for faithful Catholics, it has soured one of the most human of intimate relationships. This hard-line Roman Catholic position is but a survival from a general attitude to sex in almost all the churches – that it is unfortunately necessary for the survival of the species, but not to be encouraged for pleasure. Most churches have pulled themselves out of that abyss; but clear thinking about the role of sex in human relations and human development is hindered by this legacy.

A few years ago a young French Dominican priest was censored by the authorities in Rome for his attitude to sexuality in a book he published under the title *When I say God*. It was considered a dangerous book, and led to a very strict prohibition not to celebrate the Mass, to preach or to teach theology. He remained a Dominican, but virtually unemployed. Feeling himself "decomposing", he wrote down his experiences, hoping that "decomposition" might be followed by "composition". That book was called *God in Fragments* and in it Jacques Pohier defended his attitude to sexuality. To everyone's surprise he began with one of the most orthodox of all fountains of Catholic theology, St Thomas Aquinas. That architect of Catholic theology in his *Summa Theologica* first started Pohier on his examination of the accepted Catholic view of "virtue" as "a mastery of the will over the passions". Now Pohier found that Aquinas questioned this. He claimed that this sort of *virtue* was not the act of the will or its triumph, but that it was the expression of the passions themselves. Today the psychoanalysts would call it repression and the cause of neurosis.

Living Christianity for Pohier, as for Aquinas, thus became a recognition that the sexual relationship is part of the goodness of human nature. He even finds in Aquinas approval for seeing sex as for pleasure and not merely for procreation. So even in the Middle Ages, leading theologians were raising questions about the traditional Catholic view of sex.

I will not continue with Aquinas or Pohier. Very few today would regard sex as something wrong in itself. A virtuous life is no longer considered as one in which the passions have disappeared, nor that virtue consists in dismissing pleasure. Freud, the father of psychoanalysis, has taught us that pleasure is at the heart of human longing. The Christian view would be to see it as promoting a life in conformity with the human vocation. But we cannot leave it at that. The sexual relationship is more intimate than any other known to humankind and it is the easiest to pervert. This is why it presents us with the most serious of all our conflicts. Perhaps because of that the Catholic Church has made so much of it. The conflict lies first of all in the very potential of sexual love. It can be the highest achievement of the human person, man or woman, but it can also be degraded to a relationship as a little lower than the animals. The worst is always the best perverted. It is dangerous. For this reason it was effectively forbidden to priests, restrained in every possible way to prevent that very freedom which is its glory.

A whole culture grew up with sex as the principal sin, which should have been the highest good. Virginity was raised to a virtue. Of course, its power to destroy, which even Freud acknowledged, meant that sex had to be put under some kind of control. Without accepting the rigid Catholic view, it was necessary to define the limits of legitimate sex. But control and repression are very close. A society in which sex was officially confined to marriage led in European society to the proliferation of prostitution. A male-dominated society attempted to confine the sexual relationship to marriage for women, while an alternative was provided to relieve men of the strain of faithfulness. There were, of course, always faithful couples, who all their lives never strayed from one partner, but they were rarer than was often thought in Victorian England. In principle, sex before marriage was condemned, but it was understood if "young men sowed their wild oats", while young women were not supposed to do so. After marriage, neither was expected to stray – "until death do us part". Within such a framework there was much happiness, but much unhappiness too. The rules were broken more often than we know. The conflict comes in that sex is the natural free expression of love; while society requires a framework of restraint. Religion was used to sanction this framework. Marriage vows were for life; divorce disqualified a Christian, sometimes even from the Communion Table, certainly from ordination. The framework strained and broke.

Two world wars, the development of safe contraception, the liberation of women from a male-dominated society, the ease of divorce, and the weakening of religious sanctions, have all given us a different world. It is still not true that anything goes, but few things have changed more in our modern world than the attitude to sex. Popular entertainment reflects and encourages this free attitude. The permissive society has arrived. An older generation may watch this with mixed emotions of disapproval and envy. If they have known the good side of sexuality and loved it, they will want the next generation to love it too. They will know its dangers, but they will also know that these dangers must be accepted. Sex, like justice, truth, intelligence and faith, requires a period of experimentation. This means trial and error, which involves hard work, setbacks and suffering. How can a generation brought up with the rigid framework that continued long after the Victorian period understand that this trial and error period is not irresponsible, but perhaps necessary?

The Church – not only the Roman Catholic Church – finds this hard to accept. We cannot fully resolve this conflict yet. But many a family, believers and non-believers, are working out a pattern, less rigid, more permissive, but not necessarily less moral. When a young person decides to live with someone before getting married, we are beginning to see this as a prudent step or an understandable hesitation, rather than something fundamentally immoral. When the two partners decide to get married (often at the point when the couple consider bringing up a child together) we are beginning to see that this is a cause for celebration. A large number of Christian marriages are celebrated in this manner, where once a quiet wedding would have been advised. In this society, the conflict is there. The sexual relationship belongs to the highest moments of human life, with strong kinship with a religious act. That needs to be protected, its mystery preserved. But it is a free and very human act, which if hedged about with sanctions and prohibitions will tend to make it into a sinful act, as the Church has so often done. Christians have need to go into this world, making their contribution towards shaping the sexuality of tomorrow, with all they have to offer of the knowledge of the love of God, as made known in Jesus Christ.

Guilt

The psychiatrists have frequently accused the Church of employing methods of intimidation which develop a guilt complex, not only in sexuality, but principally there. They maintain that by imposing a guilt complex upon a person the Church prevents him or her from facing up to natural desires which have been experienced in infancy. This they say leads to repression and subsequently to a form of neurosis, which psychiatrists have to deal with on their couch. On the other hand, many Christians accuse the psychiatrists of underestimating the importance of a sense of guilt in the development of a fully human and stable character. The child who complains, "I'm maladjusted; I eat too many sweets", has clearly learnt her popular psychology as many Christians see it. Neither side is quite fair, but both have enough evidence to sustain their prejudice. Living Christianity requires understanding the nature of guilt. A life can be crippled by a persistent sense of guilt. Jesus saw this in the paralysed man who was let down from the roof by his friends, with hopes of a cure. Instead of hearing the words which his friends and the paralysed man wanted to hear – "Rise up and walk" – they heard Jesus say, "My son, your sins are forgiven". The paralysed man believed him and his life was transformed. This is not a formula for faith healing, it is a keen perception of what guilt had done to that man.

That story is a long way removed from a preacher persuading his audience that they are guilty people, who must repent before God can possibly forgive them. There is enough in the Bible and even more in subsequent Christian literature to show that an instrument for creating a sense of guilt can be constructed and put into operation with terrible consequences. Behind this instrument lies a theology of punishment for sin. God's love for us is shown in that he sent his son into the world to save sinners. But the love seems to stop there, because his awful anger against sin can be portrayed as a demand for a sacrifice (in the manner of a primitive religion) so great that only his own Son of perfect purity will do. This can be seen as referring back to the sacrifice of Isaac, when in the end God himself provided the sacrificial victim. But some theologies of the atonement have presented a fearsome God without love and bound by strict rules. Then the appeal of Christ as the victim encourages an awful sense of guilt, but does little to help one "love God". Of course, such is a misreading of the New Testament and Paul does try to put it right with "God was in Christ reconciling the world to himself". But the conflict is often there in the mind. The Christian may not always understand the theories of the atonement, but like the scientist trying to puzzle out what is going on behind the purposeful character of creation or evolution, he can see that God has acted to rescue us from the consequences of our own sin. In order to respond to this loving act of God it is necessary to recognize that we need rescuing! The proper sense of guilt, which is not paralysing but productive, can lead us to reform our ways. The Gospel, which is good news, is that God has acted to help us. The conflict is in the guilt. Does it lead us to despair, such a fear that we may have committed the unforgivable sin, that we are beyond hope; or does it make us sensitive to our need for reform? If the former, then the psychiatrist is right and we need his or her help. A guilt complex is a real and destructive thing. But if the latter, it is a healthy reaction to our own wrongdoing and we need repentance and willingness to reform. A faith in Christ makes that possible.

The traditional worship of the Church has not always helped us to resolve this conflict. So much worship consists of confession, and once the private confession had been rejected by Protestants, it mushroomed in public worship. At the Eucharist, for example, which above all worship should be a celebration, we have hardly been invited to the feast when we are cast down upon our knees to declare how sinful we are. We would never do this to guests coming to any of our house parties. What kind of Father is it who demands such behaviour at the outset of a triumphal feast? There will be time to be sad because of the cost of our salvation, the suffering of God, but confession often leads to guilt rather than praise. And after all, Eucharist simply means Thanks.

Evangelical meetings, even the best of them, so often play upon this theme of guilt. Instead of a very natural sense of having failed and needing renewal and another chance, we are often reduced to a sense of aching guilt that compels us to come forward and confess our sins. Billy Graham seems to have broken away from this kind of appeal to call for commitment to the new life, to a new relationship with God.

The conflict we have in Christian living is to reject the pathological guilt and accept the need for a proper sense of guilt for wrongdoing. In worship this probably means more thanksgiving for the joy of being alive and able to do good and human things. There needs to be a pride in human achievement to balance the real sense of inadequacy which at some times all of us feel. It is also good that Thomas

Cranmer in his draft of a General Confession for the Book of Common Prayer made us aware of the wrong we do, not only by deliberately sinful acts, but by the actions left undone. Jesus, in his parable of the Good Samaritan, gave us the phrase "passed by on the other side". The guilt we feel for things we should have done, but did not, is useful, because we can then go away and do them! Concentration upon guilt is pathological and morbid; but a sense of guilt which leads us to put things right is a wholesome corrective. But how to develop this wholesome sense of guilt without falling victim to the other is part of growing up in the life of faith.

Responsibility

Closely associated with a sense of guilt is the ability to respond to a situation in a way that improves it. When we have done wrong we take responsibility for the consequences of that wrong. The whole Judaeo-Christian view of God has this in common that "he forgives all your iniquities". Without forgiveness, the Christian way is impossible, and like love it is intertwined in three strands. God forgives us and there are a score of parables to teach us that therefore we forgive others who do us wrong. As if the parables were not clear enough, Jesus taught his disciples to pray, "Forgive us our trespasses as we forgive those who trespass against us". Then, a third strand is to forgive ourselves. Forgiveness is whole if it includes all three.

The conflict comes in deciding what our responibility is in the context of threefold love. We must respond to the situation. An act of betrayal involves at least two people. If that act is between two who love each other, it is for both to respond. The betrayer needs the forgiveness of God, the person he has betrayed and himself; but he also needs to do what is possible to put the effects of his betrayal right. He is not always able to do much, but he must not expect forgiveness to wipe out the need to do all he can to put things right. This is his proper response. The one betrayed must also examine himself (or herself) and find out whether there is anything that he or she has done to precipitate the act of betrayal. She will seek forgiveness for what she finds, from God and from the one who has betrayed her. She must also forgive herself. That enables her to forgive the betrayer. In fact, it is her (or his) proper response. This way of understanding responsibility in the context of forgiving love is to live Christianity. It has a consequence which was once pointed out by Anthony Bloom, a spiritual director in the Orthodox Church, now a Metropolitan. He said, ''Do not begin your prayers by asking God to forgive you; but begin by forgiving God''.

Facing up to the Conflicts

There are many other conflicts because life is not simple. They cannot be resolved by law, but only by love and experience. There is a need to grow in understanding of how these conflicts can be resolved in our own lives. We do not have formulae for solution. Trial and error will always play a part. Perhaps we learn more from getting it wrong than we do from always being right.

In subsequent chapters we shall look at helps and attitudes, the way of growth from confusion to some kind of confidence in living Christianity. It is a slow process and takes the best part of a lifetime. Those of us who have been on the road a long time and have therefore made most of the known mistakes rather hope that there will be time in eternity to grow a bit more. For eternity is a long time to live with yourself!

We shall look at the experience of knowing that God is there all the time. We shall try to understand the nature of real prayer, which like real ale is different from the other brands! We shall explore the extent to which the Bible is useful in our pilgrimage. We shall ask and try to answer what seems to me to be the most important question that we have to ask, "Who is Jesus Christ for us today?" We shall find out what we can about the Holy Spirit, but I warn you that he, she or it tends to have a mind of her own. In our largely secular world, which is to be welcomed and not despised, we have to find a way to worship God without denying the greatness of human achievement. Then finally, we shall look at the Church.

Whether you believe the creeds or not, may I express my personal wish for you who read this book in the words of Paul to the Ephesians:

Let the peace of Christ rule in your hearts ...
Let the word of Christ dwell in you richly.

Chapter Three

THE EXPERIENCE OF GOD
IN DAILY LIFE

If we could locate God, describe him, measure his power and perhaps plug into it for our use, we should be the gods and he our servant. It is surprising how many people do want to use God like that. After some disaster they lament, ''How can you believe in God when he allows this or that to happen?'' Of course, he has a better press when things go well! But that is not how we experience God, because all we are then doing is projecting our desires upon him and using his power to do what we cannot manage ourselves. That God is too small.

We are nearer to experiencing God when we are deeply moved by some scene of beauty or enveloped in the heavenly music of Mozart or stirred by an heroic endeavour. An act of compassion undertaken at great cost can also awaken in us a deeper sense than human admiration. I find myself describing the experience of God in terms of depth rather than height. It is not far above the bright blue sky that we experience him, but in the very depth of our being, when we are profoundly moved. The poets are best at expressing this. Wordsworth recalls a memorable morning on Westminster Bridge, 3rd September 1803, when the throbbing city of London had not yet overshadowed the mighty river that ran through it:

> Earth has not anything to show more fair!
> Dull would he be of soul who could pass by
> A sight so touching in its majesty.

This city now doth like a garment wear
The beauty of the morning: silent, bare,
Ships, towers, domes, theatres, and temples lie
Open unto the fields and to the sky;
All bright and glittering in the smokeless air.
Never did sun more beautifully steep
In his first splendour valley, rock or hill;
Ne'er saw I, never felt, a calm so deep!
The river glideth at his own sweet will:
Dear God! the very houses seem asleep;
And all that mighty heart is lying still!

A good postcard would give you all the details and rather
more, but the poet helps us to feel the impact of that beauty,
that no postcard could evoke, "Ne'er saw I, never felt, a
calm so deep". This is an experience of God, whom
Wordsworth rightly addresses. He also uses the metaphor of
depth.

The strength of that sonnet lies in the fact that we have all
felt something like that at times. They may be rare and
special times, but they are within the compass of our
experience.

The Awareness of God
This deep emotion which is aroused by love, beauty, the
endurance of a very brave person, or the self-sacrifice of a
good person, at the limit of human experience, cannot be
called an awareness of God. Those who do not share my faith
in God would resent my inference that they are experiencing
God when they are deeply moved. But this ability to respond
in the depth of our being is evidence of a human faculty that
might be compared with a sixth sense. Our other senses
enable us to hear, to smell, to see, to feel the texture of what
we touch, and to taste the sweetness and savour the

excellence of food. All five are co-ordinated to give us an overall impression, but there are moments when we experience more than this. We may call this faculty spiritual if we carefully remember that spiritual is not necessarily religious. Virtor Frankl, the Freudian who, after his experience in the concentration camps of Hitler's Germany, used his keen observation and sensitive spirit to develop out of Psychotherapy a new Logotherapy, uses the word spiritual in this wider sense. He explains the development from Freud's pleasure principle to something that might be called a will to meaning:

> A goal can be a goal of life, however, only if it has a meaning. Now, I am prepared for the argument that psychotherapy belongs to the realm of science and is not concerned with values; but I believe that there is no such thing as psychotherapy unconcerned with values. A psychotherapy which not only recognizes man's *spirit*, but actually starts from it may be termed *logotherapy*. In this connection, *logos* is intended to signify "the spiritual" and beyond that, "the meaning".

He adds an important footnote which we have to keep in mind before we too easily relate this sensitivity to an awareness of God:

> It must be kept in mind, however, that within the frame of logotherapy "spiritual" does not have a religious connotation but refers to the specifically human dimension.

The search for a meaning in what is happening to us, when we are aware of experiences far beyond our explaining by the five senses, is human. This human dimension of the spiritual is something which psychiatrists – particularly of Viktor Frankl's school and of the American practice of Humanistic Psychoanalysis associated with the name of Carl Rogers – understand better than the theologians. We religious people tend to separate human and spiritual too quickly. If then we have within our humanity a faculty which can reach out beyond the senses and experience the spiritual, we are capable of more than human efforts. Of course, this faculty can be atrophied like the other senses. A person can be deaf, blind, etc. Every effort will be made to restore the missing faculty. What then if one is deficient in the spiritual sense? Viktor Frankl once remarked, "Freud has shown us the damage done by repressing the sexual drive, but what damage is done by repressing the spiritual drives?" Does it not make sense to try to restore the spiritual faculty when it is in danger of becoming atrophied? It is reported of Darwin that he paid so much attention to details in his study of nature that he lost the sense of beauty. In one of his letters, he says as much. Should we be surprised? We all have experience of concentrating so much upon our job and efforts to succeed that when holidays come we are unable to enjoy them with the family. We cannot unwind. It is then that we need treatment, because we are losing a truly human faculty of enjoyment which has a spiritual (in the non-religious sense) quality about it. It is the element in our make up which spells the difference between pleasure and joy.

Sensitizing the Soul

How difficult it is to get away from religious language. I don't really mean anything "religious" about the word "soul". It means the true self, or in psychological terms that truly feminine part in all of us. Jonathan Porrit, who is best known for his defence of a "green" policy and his passion to preserve the beauty of the planet on which we live, was invited to do an early morning broadcast – "Prayer for the Day". He chose as his subject a poem by Gerard Manley Hopkins: "The earth is charged with the grandeur of God". He found in that poem a prayer and also a deep concern for the "bent world" which we have so sorely damaged. The poet describes the grandeur of God:

It will flame out, like shining from shook foil.

The producer asked him, "Are you aware of the presence of God?"

Jonathan lives in London and he did not have to go to some exotic place of beauty to give an example. He said he was often aware of the grandeur of God as he walked the streets and caught sight of a window box or a flower blooming in some unlikely place. It was his concern for the planet, and its survival as the green planet, that sensitized him to the presence of God. On the other hand, it is possible to become so religious that you lose this sense – so many prayers, so many church services, so many activities for good, but no resting of the mind in the presence of something greater than ourselves. Only then can we be still and know that our grasp of the world is greater than to measure and to weigh it, to assess its value or to exploit it. We can feel with a human faculty something which perhaps only a human can feel. But like all the senses it needs attention. One might compare it to learning a language. You can learn the grammar, accumulate a large vocabulary, practise fluency, but there comes a time when you know that your communication is limited by the fact that you are a stranger to the language. Your conversation becomes what you are able to talk about, rather than what most deeply concerns you. Those for whom the language is not strange make references to ideas and thoughts with which you have no contact in that language. What you have to do then is soak yourself in the literature of the culture – novels, plays, biographies, poetry – written by formative thinkers, authors to whom the language is not strange. Or it may be that you live in the country long enough to feel its burdens and share its joys. But some such experience is necessary before it is your language, in which you dream and which you use to express your deepest feelings.

It is something like this that is needed if the faculty to reach out beyond the senses is to find contact with something or someone who is at the depth of our being.

For me that someone is God, not because I am convinced by the arguments. In fact, I have never really thought of a universe without some power that I can call God, and over the years that God, whom I still find difficult to limit by the pronoun "He", has become more real and nearer. It is in this connection that I understand a rabbi's puzzlement when he was taken to see Hamlet for the first time. He said to the friend who wished to introduce him to Shakespeare's masterpiece: " ' To be or not to be'. You mean that is a question!"

If we want to reach out and find the contact with God which is possible for all, then we need to give our sixth sense a chance to dominate, if only for a few minutes. Let go of all the other five senses, neither seeing nor hearing, touching nor tasting, not even smelling, and allow ourselves to reach into the depth of our being. We shall then know that we are alive. We shall be like someone who has learnt to speak a foreign language fluently. Then the exciting quest begins. There are new territories to enter. A few examples might do at this stage, but we shall explore those territories at leisure later.

The Parable of the Fish

If fish had consciousness – and who is to say they do not – they would feel an ambiguous sense of gratitude and fear towards the water that surrounds them and from which they cannot escape on pain of death. It is the water that makes life good for them, it buoys them up, provides food, contains the air they need, neither too much nor too little. It would be clear to them that all the good things of life – "all good gifts around us" – come from this benevolent element. But also within the element lurks danger, the predators, the seductive fly of the fisher, pollution, rapids that sweep them out of control. Mother fish would explain to their children that they must treat the water with great respect, because without it they would die. I could imagine a mythology which told how the water had created all fish in the beginning and given them certain rules. If they kept these laws of the sea, then they would live. If not they would die. The laws would be for their own good. For the fish they would represent good and evil. Some fish would say that they didn't believe in the great god of the sea, that they had evolved by natural processes and all these laws were invented to keep fish in their place. The adventurous fish might even try to fly out of the water, and many would die on the bank. Older fish would explain that this happens if you break the laws of the great god of the sea. It would no doubt be those fish who managed to survive their adventures who helped evolution on to its next stage. You can play with that parable for a long time and see parallels to human endeavour, much as Kierkegaard saw parallels with human hypocrisy in the parable of the geese.

The God that Surrounds Us

The air we breathe is our water, ambiguous in much the same way. All of us are familiar with those moments of dread when we are in a totally unknown territory, lost and

47

threatened. For me the most memorable among many was in the uninhabited parts of Cambodia (Kampuchea, now). I was fascinated by the huge heads and temples of the Khmers, and wandered away from the young man who had bicycled me from one temple ruin to another. I had followed a path that seemed to trace the outline of an ancient religious procession and it led me to a magnificent head with trees growing through the eye sockets and the jungle claiming its treasure. I was too absorbed to notice that I was lost. When I realized that I had no idea how to get out of this secluded and menacing area, I recalled the maps at the hotel which had shown tiger-infested areas to be avoided. I was not sure whether I was in one of those or not. For a moment I was afraid, and the vast heads of stone seemed to afford no protection. I did not cry for help, for no one could hear me. It never occurred to me that I had to shout for God to hear. But I was acutely aware of the life in my nostrils. The air I breathed was reassuring. It filled my lungs and made me feel master of the situation. I imagine that had a tiger appeared at that moment he would have shattered my illusion. But the tiger did not appear and I felt good, alive and I could talk with God and thank him for his presence. Yes, his presence, not so much his protection. I just did not feel alone any more. I looked up at the great temple figures and enjoyed them. Slowly I walked my way back to safety. The aloneness had lasted only about two hours and yet it seemed to add a dimension to my life. I don't think I shall ever doubt that God is present after that. Without thinking I had reached out to a territory beyond the world of the senses, and I knew that God was there with me. There was crisis in that experience, but only momentary fear which may have been groundless. God surrounded me and I felt it.

The God who Holds Us Back

There are rare moments in all our lives when we are tempted to do something destructive. Our reason usually holds us back or even fear of consequences, but there are times when these are not strong enough. A wave of despair sweeps over us and we are all capable of committing suicide. A lonely hotel bedroom is dispiriting enough to weaken our defences, but if into that loneliness there comes news that in normal times we could handle, work out a way to deal with it and thwart its worst consequences, there is a temptation to self-destruction. It is cowardly and you know it, but you are alone and totally unsupported. I would never condemn a person for that self-destructive act under such circumstances. It is because we all know that in such circumstances we might do the same that we hold back from saying "coward".

In such a situation there is a resistance which resembles a power holding one back. At the time it seems like a hostile power, resisting your will. It is only in retrospect that it is seen to be a benevolent power saving your life. Suicide is the ultimate freedom. It cannot be judged before the bar of morality. You cannot say that he or she is wrong. And the old practice of refusing to bury a suicide in consecrated ground is one of the refined cruelties which religion invents from time to time.

In the moment when suicide is contemplated, whether in a desperate situation which we cannot bear to face, or during an incurable illness, or in the approaching senility of old age, we are more aware of God than at almost any other time. I do not mean fear of his punishment, but awareness of his presence holding us back and pleading with us. Because suicide is an act of unfaith. It is a lack of faith in God to do anything with what is left of our life. There is something eminently reasonable and appealing in the way in which Sigmund Freud arranged with his doctor to administer the

fatal dose of drugs when he had reached the end of his useful
life. Freud had suffered for years with a very painful disease,
and not until he was well into his eighties and he could no
longer write did he surrender. Something held even him
back, so that the world could have *Moses and Monotheism*, one
of his most important writings. I will not call that something
God, although by now Freud may know that it was. Many of
his fellow Jews, suffering appalling conditions in
concentration camps, must have felt tempted to self-
destruction, but so few did it. Those who survived, like
Viktor Frankl, whom I have already mentioned; Bruno
Bettelheim, who later developed an outstanding work among
autistic children in Chicago; Primo Levi, whose writings in
Italian have helped us to understand the terrible importance
of the concentration camps and Hitler's genocide; they have
all faced this moment and been held back. Primo Levi
eventually, like Freud, surrendered. But not before he had
written *The Drowned and the Saved*, as a climax to a whole
series of illuminating novels about the camps. He had to live
to tell his story, and he expresses his compulsion in words
from Coleridge's *Rime of the Ancient Mariner*:

> Since then, at an uncertain hour,
> That agony returns
> And till my ghastly tale is told
> This heart within me burns

which he puts as a dedication to his last book. That
compulsion held him back, and so did the exchange of letters
with a German woman who understood his destiny. When
the tale was told and his German companion had died, he
claimed the right to self-destruction.

The Daily Round

So many stories about the presence of God surrounding us and holding us back are of exotic places or extreme situations. That is inevitable in a culture which hardly bothers about or reports good news. I have given my exotic stories, now the daily round, the common task. Where then is God? Has he a word for the bored, the tired, the ordinary lives? It is hard, when nothing relieves the dull routine, to find God in the household tasks or overheated offices. The dullness of life is very naturally tackled by more and more exotic holidays, exciting TV, even "Dallas" and "Neighbours". But this has the old name of escapism. When the holiday is over and the TV switched off, life, with its pressures unrelieved by the heavenly vision, can find it hard to think of God, or even imagine him there in the kitchen or the office. I suppose it was for that reason that wonderful churches were built, great music composed to lift the magnificent words of the Liturgy into the heavenlies. But that is to make an idol of God, or at least to undermine his influence upon our daily lives. Church, like exotic holidays, can also be a form of escapism. Jonathan Porritt found God in a window box; Gerard Manley Hopkins in "shook foil"; George Herbert found words for it:

> Teach me, my God and King,
> In all things Thee to see,
> And what I do in anything
> To do it as for Thee.
>
> A man that looks on glass
> On it may stay his eye;
> Or if he pleaseth, through it pass,
> And then the heaven espy.

All may of Thee partake;
Nothing can be so mean,
Which with this tincture, "For Thy sake",
Will not grow bright and clean.

A servant with this clause
Makes drudgery divine;
Who sweeps a room, as for Thy laws,
Makes that and the action fine.

This is the famous stone
That turneth all to gold:
For that which God doth touch and own
Cannot for less be told.

George Herbert lived at the beginning of the seventeenth
century, and we must make allowance for the social values of
his time. But that old-fashioned poem has truth in it still.
There are many who lift up the common task because they
are doing it for others, even earning a living for their family.
In the days of mass production when Charlie Chaplin made
his great film, *Modern Times*, I knew a man who, when asked
how he could possibly endure a soul-destroying job of
making the same motion as he tightened a piece of
machinery exactly the same way a thousand times a day,
replied from deep conviction: "When I bend my arms, I say
with the poetry of a conductor of a great orchestra, I am
building a home. That makes all the difference. It is not soul-
destroying repetition, it is building a family and a home."
When your motive is noble enough, the action is
transformed. And that is what George Herbert is talking
about. Many who sing the hymn to the traditional English
carol tune of "Sandys" never think of the transforming
power of "as for Thy laws". But there are others who never
sing the hymn, but know the transformation wrought by
God's presence in daily routine work. It does not have to be

creative work, which perhaps does not need transforming. It is in dull work that the presence of God is most effective.

For the God who surrounds us is not a religious God, not necessarily an artistic or creative God, but one who is there in the secular and unimaginative things of life.

Death and Beyond

A great deal more sense is talked about death than when I was young, when the subject was as taboo as sex and money. All such taboos in conversation have now gone, and death was the last to fall. The monument to that last taboo is the hospice movement, where people talk freely about their own death and seek to accomplish it in dignity. There are two fears about death that I meet consistently: the fear of senility before death and the fear of being alone. Science and human understanding have done much to ease the onset of senility, in some cases removing it altogether.

The aloneness is more difficult to handle, and is still the most prevalent fear among many people who have chosen to live alone in their own flat to the end. Not everyone can die in a hospice, but the glorious achievement of the hospice movement has been that no one there dies alone. The patient is surrounded with care and that helps to ease the pain. So often on my visits to people in a hospice I have found the peace of being part of that community to the end. That peace enables the dying person to talk about death and speculate about what lies beyond, as well as trying to prepare loved ones for the future. So often a woman has said to me, "I am quite happy about dying. I know it will not be long. But I wish you would talk to my husband. He obstinately insists that I am going to get better. He will not face the fact that I am dying." She realizes that it would be so much easier for her if he would. In a perfect society, all old people would spend their last months in a hospice, surrounded by care.

But friends and helpers can only accompany you so far. The last step is taken alone. And what lies beyond that last step? The body is finished, the brain has ceased to function. But a person is not only body and brain. There is an essence which we call the self or the soul. It cannot be located in the body any more than God can be located in space. It is of different substance from the physical.

What happens to that person after death? He or she continues in the memory of their friends. But is that all? Does the continuing life cease when our friends have forgotten us? The Christian believes that a relationship with people and with God can survive physical death. The word "survival" has a declining value about it. The Christian talks rather of resurrection. It is a pity that for so long we have talked of "the resurrection of the body". There is nothing in the New Testament to suggest that the body which served us in life will come back and be used again. Most of us, by the time we reach death, have had enough of that body anyway!

What Did Jesus Say about Death and Beyond?
Early Christians were insistent that what happened to Jesus was vital for an understanding of what will happen to us when we die. They built all kinds of theories on that conviction, which are not important, but the conviction is. They believed the first witnesses who said that without a shadow of doubt, Jesus was seen alive after his crucifixion. The stories they told all had to do with their relationship with him. Some of the most colourful stories in the gospels are of these resurrection appearances – by the lakeside when they were fishing, on the road when they were travelling, in the garden when a woman had lost her loved one, at table during a meal, and so on. Always they insisted this meant that they would never be separated from him. But he also said

something about life after death which was remembered, although probably not in the words he actually used. We are dependent upon their understanding of his words and the interpretation they put upon them, and to which a subsequent generation added. That makes it sound all a bit vague and remote, but it is what always happens with any tradition. Anybody writing today about the Second World War is about as distant from the event itself as the gospel writers were from the life of Jesus. The Fourth Gospel, which is the one that says most about life after death with Jesus, was about as distant as we are from the First World War. Rather more time to add a bit of comment to what he really said. But, despite all that, there is a ring of truth about these accounts in the gospels. In the Fourth Gospel (i.e. "John"), there are three chapters which attempt to piece together what Jesus said about his departure, that is, his death. He was apparently trying to cheer them up. One had said that he wanted to die too. This often happens with a close group of idealists: their leader is to die and they want to go with him. Jesus warns Peter that he will not stand the test, but will fail at the crucial moment, as indeed he did. Then he goes on to say that they will all follow later. Of course, they will all die eventually, but that is not what he means. He describes his death as a journey, and himself as the leader of a party who goes ahead to prepare the way. They follow like pilgrims and find that they are expected at every point they reach. He calls that realm or state of existence beyond death "My Father's House", and compares it to a territory where God rules. Jesus urges them not to allow the relationship with him to be broken. To help them maintain this he promises that his spirit will be with them. This "spirit" is defined as a "Comforter" (i.e. one who stands by your side) or "Counsellor". It is the continuing influence of Jesus for them and will carry them through until they enter his

Father's realm. We then have the text of a prayer which he prays for his disciples and for those who will believe because of their witness. He prays that they might be left in the world, but protected from "the evil one".

These chapters in the Fourth Gospel have comforted many Christians who were afraid, as death approached, that all was to be snuffed out.

There is not much point in trying to speculate about heaven or hell, though that won't stop people doing it. The furniture of heaven and the temperature of hell have a continuing fascination! But it is unprofitable. We don't know. Yet for a Christian there is a relationship built up with God, whom we know as our heavenly Father through Jesus, which somehow cannot be broken by death. We enter a new territory after death, but not a foreign one; we take nothing with us, not even our bodies, but we remain ourselves. In the simple language of Paul the Apostle, "God gives us another body", and this is not physical, but spiritual. The awareness of God remains.

Chapter Four

WHEN PRAYER BECOMES REAL

The awareness of God, of which all humans are capable, grows throughout our life. It can be a little odd at first, a feeling that you would rather not talk about. Gradually it changes until you feel, not so much that you are aware of God, but that God is aware of you. It is then that some kind of response is called for. That response is prayer.

For prayer to be real and not just the repetition of sacred words, there has to be some recognition that God notices you and is in fact searching for you. That wonderful poem of Francis Thompson describes the search as like "The Hound of Heaven" pursuing and he runs away in fear, until,

> Halts by me that footfall;
> Is my gloom after all
> Shade of his hand, outstretched caressingly?
> "Ah, fondest, blindest, weakest;
> I am he whom thou seekest!
> Thou dravest love from thee, who dravest Me."

That experience of running away from God until you realize that he means you no harm, but simply desires your good, is a widespread experience, even though few can put it into lines as moving as those of Francis Thompson. Its successful climax is the recognition that God searches for us long before we are aware of him. The Bible is full of such statements as,

Before I formed you in the womb I knew you, and before you were born I consecrated you; I appointed you a prophet to the nations.

Our awareness of God comes when we recognize this. The American preacher and writer, H. E. Fosdick, put it quite clearly:

God is for ever seeking each man. Finding God is really letting God find us. When the truth of this is clearly seen, Prayer becomes real.

Prayer is a creative response to that recognition.

How Can We Learn to Pray?

When his disciples asked Jesus to teach them to pray, he did eventually give them a prayer which they could use, although I think it was only intended to be an example helping us to find our own words. Matthew, who gives us an account of this incident, says that before giving them that prayer Jesus cleared out of the way three wrong ways to pray:

1. Don't make a show of it. Prayer is a very personal thing and your response must be to God, not to bystanders. Pray to God in secret, he said.

2. Prayer is not talk, which, however beautiful, stands in danger of becoming empty phrases. Prayer is not made effective because of the words used.

3. Don't think you are telling God anything he doesn't know already. "Your Father knows what you need before you ask him."

After he has given them a model prayer, he adds another warning against false prayer:

4.   Don't think your prayer has ended when you open your eyes and get off your knees. The whole of your life is your prayer.

In the model prayer not much was asked – "daily bread" and forgiveness. Most of the prayer is about wanting to be close to God and to share in his rule or kingdom, wanting his will to be done and hoping not to get lost to the evil one. Asking for forgiveness is qualified in words that, even to this day, Christians get a little uneasy about:

> And forgive us our debts,
> *as we also* have forgiven our debtors.

Matthew tells us that he didn't leave it at that, but drove it home with "For if you forgive men their trespasses, your heavenly Father also will forgive you; but if you do not forgive men their trespasses, neither will your Father forgive your trespasses".

That comment puts prayer right into life. Prayer is a recognition of the "Hound of Heaven" and a response in the whole of life.

So it might be well to look at those warnings a little before proceeding to ways in which we learn to pray.

The first concerns the intimacy of prayer. Of course, there are public prayers and ceremonial prayers, as when a king or queen is crowned, or at national days. These are the public expression of a deep feeling which many people have in common. A congregation of people prays. This is not what we are looking at when we ask how *we* can learn to pray. We can all, without much learning, be swept along by a praying congregation or a national emotion – for example, the relief of Dunkirk, when it looked as though the entire British Army of the Rhine would be wiped out or taken prisoner. Whether we regard that as a providential act, or sheer good luck that the weather made evacuation possible, or the superb courage of the little boats, we can feel gratitude which needs to be expressed publicly. This common emotion may explain an odd result from a statistical survey I saw some years ago. It was in the early 'fifties, and the Audience Research Department of the BBC conducted its first survey of religious opinion and practice. An extraordinary number of people affirmed that they believed in God – about 80 per cent, I think – but the church-going was a great deal lower. The extraordinary figure was the number who affirmed that they prayed. There were more who prayed than believed in God. This is not prayer as the Christian would understand it. And yet, I am not sure. Is the cry, "O God!" a prayer? George MacDonald, who was one of the most influential forces in the life of C.S. Lewis, expresses very strongly his view that it is the basis of all prayer, and there is truth in his comment:

> " O God", I cried, and that was all. But what are the prayers of all the universe more than expansions of that one cry? It is not what God can give us, but God that we want.

And that is certainly true. Prayer, if it is a recognition that God is seeking us, is a longing for the God who seeks.

That quote from George MacDonald also fits the second warning: "do not heap up empty phrases as the Gentiles do; for they think that they will be heard for their many words ... "

The Church has often forgotten that warning. The beautifully phrased prayers of the Shakespearian age, the familiar cadences of Cranmer's Prayer Book, the penetrating rebukes of modern writers of prayers, have so often been recommended as models. Yet, they are words, however well and cleverly phrased. Sometimes they may exactly fit our mood and help us to respond to God. Sometimes they are effective in bringing together a whole congregation in words they know and love. But these are the outward trimmings of prayer, real enough in their way, but without meaning unless personal prayer is behind them.

Real prayer often needs no words at all. It is like Leonardo sitting in front of the canvas on which he was to paint the Last Supper waiting for the face of Christ to appear. The onlookers cried, "He is doing nothing. He is idle. He is wasting his time. He is defrauding his patron."

But Leonardo was doing the most important part of his painting. He was waiting, receptive. When he saw the face, the rest was technique. So with prayer, the words are the least important – the technique, no more. It is said of St Francis of Assisi that one of his closest admirers hid in his cell to hear what words he must use in prayer to bring forth such saintliness. All he heard St Francis say was, "Jesus, my Jesus".

The third warning has come already: don't think you're telling God anything he does not know already. You can of course tell yourself things in the presence of God, and they may sound different! Even human communication would be a poor thing if it depended only upon words. But we use words.

The fourth warning is about the use of those words. They must be noted well, because you have to live them. In the First Letter of John in the New Testament, there is a very blunt statement which emphasizes how fragile words are, even in prayer:

If any one says, "I love God", and hates his brother,
he is a liar (4:20).

And Jesus' fourth warning says much the same. Don't ask
forgiveness unless you are prepared to forgive. Prayer
exposes the whole of life to the judgement of God. A
Christian soon discovers, to use the words of an old prayer,
that God is the one "to whom all hearts be open, all desires
known and from whom no secrets are hid".

The Rope of Coloured Strands

Prayer is a very human activity, and yet it develops faculties
in us which respond to our strange awareness of God and
takes us out of the purely human sphere, although never
permanently, just caught up for a while. Prayer always
brings us down to earth – with or without a bump. It
permeates everything we do, and grows so that we are never
quite free of it. Every act is a prayer and every prayer an act.

It was Olive Wyon who first introduced me to the idea of
thinking about prayer as a rope of four coloured strands,
black, yellow, red and blue, woven and twisted together. She
got the image from Leonard Boase of the Society of Jesus,
and it has spread a long way since then into all the various
traditions of Christian faith and practice. From Jesuits to
Baptists is quite a long way, and somehow it rings true
despite all our prejudices against each other. That
encourages me to believe that the Church will be united not
by theological discussions, nor by administrative
negotiations, but by prayer. We all draw upon one another's
experience and ideas in the practice of prayer.

But let me get back to that rope, and its four coloured
strands.

The black strand is the background to all the rest. It is
work, our daily task, what we have to do to earn our living,

whether we like it or not. It is our duty. The experience of unemployment or even the fear of it soon shows us how much work gives strength and stability to our lives. That job can be offered to God, which may make all the difference to the way we do it. We would not offer to God that which costs us nothing, nor work which has been done carelessly or without concern for our fellow workers. Our solidarity with our fellow workers may lead us to strike, and if this is carefully considered and undertaken for the achieving of just treatment, that too can be offered to God. This is the basic strand of our prayer – our duty.

The yellow strand is *play*, everything we do because we want to, because we like it. This covers recreation, artistic, scientific, literary or domestic activities which we do for pleasure. Because we offer this relaxed activity to God we exercise a measure of self-control. That control and selection does not in any way detract from the pleasure, but rather enhances it as the rules make a game more enjoyable. Thus, play becomes an ordered development of ourselves in a realm where we have chosen to do what we find pleasure in.

The red strand is *sacrifice*, which covers everything we would rather not choose, from the small mishaps and disappointments to the profound suffering which at times drives us to distraction. It includes the things we give up for the sake of a closer relationship with God or with those we love. There is no life without renunciation, but what determines our development or regression is how we react to the renunciations imposed upon us. We have all seen people destroyed by disappointments, and others made strong in mind and will by tragedy. Some lives appear to have more than their share of tragedy, while others seem to escape any serious deprivation. The extent of the tragedy is not what matters, but the acceptance and use of it. This can be prayer at its most profound; tragedy or failure offered to God.

The blue strand is what is usually called *prayer*. Leonard Boase says of this strand that it is "loving God through some sort of awareness, attention which is directed to Him, loving Him through thinking about Him." This is the strand which binds them all into a unity.

In the first three strands we are relating our life to God, praying by intention, trying to do God's will in every part of our life. This does not mean that at work, at play and in our suffering we are constantly thinking of God. It means that our work and our play and our suffering are all related to God's will for us and our desire to please Him.

The fourth strand is quite different. It is *praying by attention*, withdrawing from other activities to concentrate our attention on God. All four strands are interwoven but it is necessary to see the difference between the first three, which are a *state* of prayer, and the fourth, which is the activity of prayer itself, untroubled by other activities. The state of prayer is fundamental, because without it "pure prayer" is not possible. But the fourth requires definite planning, whether for a long period or a brief moment. We have to make time for this prayer and make it regularly. It does not have to be long, but without it the three other strands disentangle.

The Golden String

Prayer is not simply a personal activity. It is a way of relating to other people at a very profound level. Bede Griffiths, a Roman Catholic monk who has spent much of his life in South India, recounts how he discovered real prayer on his first visit to a monastery:

> Prayer had always been for me something private and apart, something of which one would never dream of speaking to anyone else. But now I found myself in an

atmosphere where prayer was the breath of life. It was accepted as something as normal as eating and drinking. I shall never forget my surprise when someone told me quite casually that he would pray for me; the supernatural world suddenly became for me something positive and real, something quite matter-of-fact. I realized now what it was that I had missed all the time. It was the absence of prayer as a permanent background to life which made modern life so empty and meaningless. Life in the modern world was cut off from its source in God; men's minds were shut up in the confines of the material world and their own personalities, unable to escape from their fetters. Here the mind was kept open to God, and everything was brought into relation with Him. I had caught a glimpse ...

That was in a monastery, and it must be stressed that what he had glimpsed is not confined to monastic life. In a more vibrant way it can be transposed to a workaday world. The monastery simply provides laboratory conditions. Monastic rules nearly always include a measure of controlled manual work, orderly activity and, apart from enclosed orders, lively contact with those outside its walls. The monks are no more holy than other Christians, but they live an ordered life under conditions similar to the scientists' laboratory. That is why retreats are of help to those working in a busy world. Bede Griffiths found this on his first visit, and later became a monk. His writings are of particular value to those of us trying to live Christianity, because his laboratory was extended beyond the Western monastic system to South India, where for much of his life he has studied and demonstrated the value of prayer and meditation. Those who have been to his ashram have come away, not determined to be monks and nuns, but to live in the world.

The Golden String is his autobiography, and a reading of it helps any person to find a way to prayer, not by imitation, but by discovery. The title comes from Blake's poem:

> I give you the end of a golden string;
> Only wind it into a ball,
> It will lead you in at heaven's gate,
> Built in Jerusalem's wall.

One of the discoveries is that prayer is a communal activity, linking us with those for whom we pray and who pray with us. It depends upon an inner centre of prayer where we can meet with one another in the presence of God. Here is how Bede Griffiths explains that:

> It is only in prayer that we can communicate with one another at the deepest level of our being. Behind all words and gestures, behind all thoughts and feeling, there is an inner centre of prayer where we can meet one another in the Presence of God. It is this inner centre which is the real source of life and activity and of all love ... Here alone can all the conflicts of this life be resolved, and we can experience a Love which is beyond time and change.

That may be learnt in a monastery, but it has to be lived in the daily life of every Christian in the world. It provides a great source of strength and reserve for one busily engaged in the bustle of life. I have known several monks in my time, and almost all of them have been very competent people when it came to handling the affairs of business and administration. The present Cardinal Archbishop of Westminster, Basil Hume, is a very good example. These laboratory conditions enable those who will to explore the inner resources of the human *pysche*, and observe as they practise the life of prayer. This is not only in Christian monasticism. Hermann Hesse, in his novel about the Buddha, *Siddartha*, takes the young monk who has disciplined himself in the forest, into the wordly affairs of business and sexual relationships. He shows that the skills learnt in monastic life are precisely those needed in worldly life. So we should observe closely what is learnt in the monastery, either by reading or visiting. These things are as important to those who wish to live Christianity as a research laboratory can be to our industry.

Jesus as a Master of Prayer

If we lay aside the claims that are made about Jesus – that he was the Son of God, born of a virgin, rose from the dead, ascended into heaven – not because these claims are unimportant, but because they often get in the way of our understanding his life, we may observe the way in which he lived Christianity. In particular, we can observe how he prayed and the effect of prayer upon him. The gospels portray a real person, who spoke with the deepest sincerity. Although he saw that many people did not know what to do with their lives, he most certainly knew what to do with his own. He saw the ravages of anxiety in so many lives, but his own heart was at peace. He spoke of God as one he knew. People were amazed at the confidence with which he spoke of spiritual things. As W.R. Maltby, in his book *The Significance of Jesus*, writes, "in hours, more sacred than we can conceive, [He Himself] had entered into the inner chamber, shut the door, and found the Father." In the nature of things there can be no report of what he said verbatim, but the gospel writers who listened to those who knew him intimately, wrote what they imagined he must have said.

They had to explain what it was that lay behind his poise and calmness. They deduced that it came from a lifetime of prayer, and what he said confirmed this. In childhood, youth and manhood, which he had spent in Nazareth in a carpenter's home, he learnt to pray, and his familiarity with God was one of the most evident things about him.

Later, his disciples observed that in crowded days of healing, teaching and helping people, he withdrew to pray. That withdrawal is often described. The gospel writers tell of a time at the beginning of his ministry when he withdrew to the wilderness, and for a long time wrestled with himself in the company of nature, without human companions. It was his monastery. A strange dialogue is recorded with the evil one. In the mythology of the day, Jesus is shown as seeking to discover who he was and how he should use the power he evidently had in his person. He rejected three misuses of power. If his mission was to declare the coming of the rule of God into the world, he would need to rally people to his side to oppose the alternative rule of evil. In the temptation to turn stones into bread because he was hungry, he was being asked to become a worker of miracles. If he had the power to do it, why did he not feed hungry Palestine? Such questions we might ask of God today when we learn of hunger, malnutrition and starvation in Africa and Asia. The gospels tell of two incidents when he fed a multitude and they wanted to make him king. Surely he would have rallied all men to his side if he had by miracles done all the things they longed to do, but could not: feed the hungry, heal the sick, raise the dead. All these things came into his ministry later, but this was not his message to the world. The message was to recognize the goodness of God, not the privileges of those who join up. He rejected too the spectacular miracle of jumping from the pinnacle of the temple. Trust in God is one thing, but testing his willingness to help by foolish ventures is not the way to help people understand God. Those two temptations are wide-spread enough still. They must be met by prayer, and Jesus found his answers in the Bible, words that expressed what he knew to be true:

> Man shall not live by bread alone.
>
> Thou shall not test the Lord Thy God.

Christianity is not a religion of miracles, although many would make it such. There are miracles enough, but they are of the transforming of people, many of whom make hunger their prayer, and diligently work to serve themselves and their neighbours without resorting to supernatural aid. God is not a divine giver of hand-outs.

The third temptation was of a different kind, but once again Jesus faced it in prayer. What do you do to win the world? Compromising with those forces which are against the rule of God, even though at present they hold the power and have the largest array, is a recipe for disaster.

"Worship me!", says the evil one, "I have the whole world in my hands." It often looks as though he has. Jesus was soon to face the power of that evil in the authorities who could stand him no longer and so destroyed him – as they might destroy a fly. If he had been more accommodating the Sanhedrin would have been behind him. His integrity was at stake that moment in the wilderness. He fell back upon his childhood religion:

> Thou shalt worship the Lord thy God and him only shalt thou serve!

Prayer is a wrestling with our problems, our temptations, our schemes and ideas, in the presence of God. It is worth reading the account of these temptations, if only to discover how near they are to our own. "He was tempted in all points like we are", but in prayer he won through.

The Ultimate Prayer

All four gospels spend a major part of their story on the last week of the life of Jesus and the subsequent resurrection appearances. Great importance is given to the manner of his death and, of course, the resurrection was the beginning of their proclamation. The first declaration of the gospel is quite simply, "He is risen!" But in those seven days leading up to the crucifixion each evangelist describes every detail and makes quite clear that the disciples were confused. Only the resurrection made sense of his death, for them. So the details are not those of an historian but of preachers, and everything that happened was seen in the light of the resurrection. All agree that the Last Supper was an occasion for learning. It was sad, darkened by ominous forebodings and sickened by betrayal. It acquired its meaning after the resurrection. But one incident remains, untouched by any interpretation after the event and it remains poignant and puzzling, but real. It is after the Last Supper when they had sung a hymn and gone out into the darkness. Jesus needed time for prayer, and he set three disciples on guard to secure quietness and prevent interruption. They slept on duty. But they talked later of that time with shame and understanding. Denis Potter, in his TV life of Jesus, linked that prayer with the Temptations. He was still asking, "Who am I?" The prayer was a request, it had few words and it ended in acceptance:

Father, if it be possible, let this cup pass from me.

He was afraid, he wanted to be sure that it was all necessary, he needed to know if there was another way. Although this was a unique moment in the history of prayer, it bears enough resemblance to our own dilemmas in prayer to be helpful. We believe that the God who loves us can hear our reluctance and understand our fears. He is not unmoved by our longing for an easier way. There is a story told of Jacob in the Old Testament which is a kind of primitive Gethsemane, and we can understand him. He was a cheat, he stole his brother's birthright, he fooled his blind old father, and he ran for his life from his brother Esau. Years later, when both were prosperous, Jacob feared to meet his brother, and by the river Jabbok wrestled with God in a dream. He wanted to avoid meeting Esau, he was afraid. God insisted that Jacob had no choice. But when he met his brother, he saw his face as though it were the face of God.

Jesus triumphed already in the prayer with the acceptance of his Father's will, knowing the consequences and facing them bitterly. All this lay before him as he uttered the supreme ultimate prayer:

> Nevertheless, Thy will, not mine be done.''

It was not an easy prayer and it never is, but it is the goal to which all prayer aims.

Meister Eckhart

Johannes Eckhart was born in Hochheim, Rhineland in 1260. He was a Dominican preacher and a profound mystical writer who believed in teaching the common people, as did England's John Wycliffe nearly a century later. When others complained that Eckhart was teaching things that the common people might not really understand and could lead them into error, he replied:

> If the ignorant are not taught they will never learn, and

none of them will ever know the art of living and dying. The ignorant are taught in the hope of changing them from ignorant to enlightened people.

Wycliffe would have agreed, because both were concerned to break the false dominance of the Church. Eckhart had a way with his teaching and he explains the "ultimate prayer" in words worth quoting:

> The most powerful prayer, one well-nigh omnipotent, and the worthiest work of all is the outcome of a quiet mind. The quieter it is the more powerful, the worthier, the deeper, the more telling and the more perfect the prayer is. To the quiet mind all things are possible. What is a quiet mind? A quiet mind is one which nothing weighs on, nothing worries, which, free from ties and all self-seeking, is wholly merged into the will of God and dead to its own. Such an one can do no deed however small but it is clothed with something of God's power and authority.

The final prayer of Jesus, which the disciples said was "with great drops of blood", was a prayer of meek acquiescence, but of triumph:

> Nevertheless, Thy will, not mine be done.

Chapter Five

THE STRANGE RELEVANCE OF THE BIBLE

Christians are not the only people who believe in God. All the earliest Christians were Jews, and they inherited a passionate belief in One God. There is no argument about whether God exists or not in the Bible. James, one of the New Testament writers, lays it on the line in a letter which is particularly frank: "You believe that there is only one God. Good! Even the demons believe that." The Muslims also believe in God. The Buddhists may be a bit uncertain, but they are really a reforming sect of Hinduism, which has gods in plenty, although most Hindus recognize a superior god. The African traditional religions, and that of the Amero-Indians, which is sometimes called "animism" because of a multiplicity of spirits, retain belief in one Great Spirit, above them all, who might be likened to God.

What is peculiar about Christians is *what* they believe about God and *how* they relate to God.

This is set out in a doctrinaire way in the historic Creeds – Apostles', Nicene, etc. But those creeds are a bit cold, and they have been so much misused to keep people out, that they do not convey the feeling of a loving relationship to a loving God. A much better guide is the Bible.

This was recognized in England at the time of the Reformation. There were interminable arguments about the writing of "Articles" which defined the faith and practice of the Church of England, but what came through to most people was a threefold source of authority:

a)   Christians were not compelled to believe that which was against reason;

b)   The experience and knowledge of centuries of the Christian Church could not be disregarded;

c)   The Bible had acquired an authority which was not defined very clearly, but which was universally accepted.

The Strange Composition of the Bible

More than three-quarters of the Bible used by Christians is inherited from the Jews. The Old Testament was taken over just as it was, the Bible on which most of the earliest Christians had been nourished. Even the New Testament, which is the Christian contribution, is written by people brought up as Jews, with the exception of Luke.

The Old Testament is itself a collection of writings over a period of a thousand years. The first five books, not by any means the earliest, are collections of stories, laws, memorable sayings and warnings that cover a long period. They are put together and called *The Torah*, which means more than *The Law*, but remains the authority for all Jews. The rest of the Old Testament is divided by the Jews into two parts. There is first what is called *The Prophets*; that includes an account of Israel's history, guided by God, and a series of books bearing the names of individuals who spoke to the nation in the name of God, Prophets like Isaiah, Jeremiah, Ezekiel, and a dozen lesser known spokesmen. The third part is called *The Writings* which includes several books of Psalms, gathered together into one, a few books of poetry, proverbs, stories and moral tales. One gets the impression that most Jews regard them in descending order of authority. The Torah is supreme; the Prophets help you to understand it in the setting of different historical periods; the Writings are for edification.

These three parts formed the basis of the Christian Bible,

which did not clearly distinguish between them. All became known as The Word of God. Of course, Christians read them differently, seeing the figure of Christ on every page. Even that religio-erotic collection of poems called *The Song of Songs* was interpreted as the love of Christ for his Church. And almost every unfulfilled prophecy of a prophet, as well as some of those already fulfilled, was interpreted as showing the coming of Christ. The Greek-speaking Jews had already enlarged their Bible by a series of extra books and stories, which Christians took over, giving them a little less authority, although to be read for edification. These are what we call the *Apocrypha*.

So Christians inherited a history and a holy book. In fact, for some time they even worshipped with Jews in their synagogue, and while it still stood, they went up to the Jewish Temple to pray.

But Christians had something else to say about God. They said that Jesus of Nazareth, a man who went about preaching, much along the lines of John the Baptist, working miracles of healing and doing good, was God's man as foretold in the Bible. They collected texts from the Law, the Prophets and the Psalms to show that he was promised. Their evidence was that, although rejected and crucified, he rose from the dead. This converted some Jews to their way of thinking, but even more non-Jews. Quarrels arose and the Christians split away from the Jewish synagogues. In Christian churches they worshipped and taught many things identical with the Jews, but they added stories that the first disciples told and sometimes wrote down about their personal experiences with this Jesus – his miracles and his teaching. Gradually all the disciples were dying off and what they wrote was collected together – letters sent to churches or even individuals. Later, gospels were written to tell the life, death and resurrection of Jesus. Some of the letters, particularly those written by Paul, worked out a theology of the Christian religion. Paul tried to show how the death of Christ delivered us, like slaves set free, from our sins. He also developed a vision of how the Christians, as children of God, would pioneer the renewal of the world, not only for people, but for animals and all creation.

The central event for the early Christians seems to have been the resurrection. They pinned all their hopes on that. But soon new converts wanted to know more about the person of Jesus, and hence the popularity of the gospels. The first three were dependent upon one another – Mark was probably written first, about thirty years after the crucifixion. Matthew and Luke, some twenty years later than Mark, knew his gospel and used it as a basic framework for their own. They both found it necessary to add something about his birth. No doubt, questions were asked, such as: "If he was the Son of God, surely something supernatural must have happened at his birth?" So birth stories, from whatever source, were added. They have given us all the Christmas legends! Much more of the teaching of Jesus was collected by Matthew, and more of the parables by Luke. Taken together, the three gospels (usually called the Synoptic Gospels, because they can be compared in parallel columns) give us a lot of information about the life and teaching of Jesus. They also, apart from Mark, give us a rich array of resurrection stories, which were already circulating among Christians at the time. Paul listed them in one of his Letters before any gospel was written.

The Fourth Gospel is much later, and has been given the name of "John". It is quite different from the other three, being more carefully composed, not to provide a portrait or mini-biography, but a study of the meaning of it all. Each chapter usually begins with a story and then goes on to draw out its meaning. The whole gospel is structured around a series of what are called "signs", designed to indicate who Jesus was and to inspire worship.

The Gospel itself explains why it was written. The writer says that he could have written a lot more, but what he had written was "that you may believe that Jesus is the Christ, the Son of God, and that believing you may have life in his name".

Luke's Gospel is the only one that had a sequel (The Acts of the Apostles). In this he continued the story of the life of Jesus by writing an account of the early Church, led by the Holy Spirit to witness to Christ, and he followed the mission of Paul into all the world. Luke probably intended to write a third book.

Finally there is the strange Book of the Revelation. It purports to be a vision of the last days and the triumph of the Church when Christ returns in glory. It belongs to the class of apocalyptic literature popular at that time among the Jews and is often called, "The Apocalypse".

Looked at in this way, historically, the Bible appears to be an unlikely book to guide anyone through the twentieth century. The scientific worldview is unknown to its authors or to the players in the drama. But for a long time, most Christians simply took it as a religious book and found much wisdom in it. There are matters of daily life and human relationships which do not depend much upon worldviews, but rather upon the wealth of human experience. And the very nature of the biblical material is such that you can enter into it and feel the pulses of moral decisions. It is, on the whole, not to be quoted, like the Koran, as the unanswerable will of God. Lifting texts out of their context can become quite ridiculous. You could even declare, "There is no God", because that is also in the Bible.

The Strange Relevance

In an Indian village in the 'fifties, when laws were being passed to set villagers free from the tyranny of money-lenders, and peasants were beginning to work their own land, I discovered a strange relevance in one of the Christian villages. The money-lenders had insisted that the people could not work their land until they had paid their debts. This was not legal, and the villagers could have taken the money-lenders to court and won their case. A young radical was anxious that they should do that and roused support to make it possible. But the Christian villagers had been reading the story of Abraham and Lot. Abraham and his nephew, Lot, journeyed from their home with all their servants and cattle, nomads until they came to the land God had appointed for them. Abraham was the leader of the caravan, and as they came to the land where they were to settle, they saw on the one hand, rich fertile soil, on the other, hard hill country. The two households quarrelled and had to divide. Abraham allowed Lot to choose which way he would go. Lot, of course, chose the fertile land and left his uncle with the hard, hilly land. As the villagers studied this, they saw that Abraham had chosen the possibility of good relations in the future rather than advantage in the present. They considered their own situation. The eleven Christian villages would have to live side by side with the richer money-lenders. Although they had the right to maintain their legal refusal to repay the debts, they decided to work harder and repay the debts to continue in good relation with their richer Hindu neighbours. The old story was very relevant for them. They understood Abraham's dilemma and learnt from it.

In a quite different and rather more sophisticated way the Christians of Germany learnt how to judge the wrongs of the Hitler regime by a careful and honest study of the Bible. For twelve years it was all they had to help them judge right and wrong in a system which controlled every form of decision-making, from newspapers to universities. They did not look up texts, but carefully studied Bible passages in their historical setting and laid them side by side with similar issues upon which they had to decide in the Germany of their day.

When we look at issues of topical concern today, it is often extremely difficult to decide which is the right course – peace and war, nuclear energy, food production, profit and wages, house purchase, investments etc. Few of them have exact parallels in the Bible, but when the issue is analysed down to its basic conflicts we are often able to find an equivalent story in the scriptures, which although in a totally different culture raises the same conflicts. In the biblical narratives we find not only the consequences of actions taken in such situations, but also detect the presence of God in the decisions. The ancient documents may express this in terms of punishment and reward which are not acceptable to us, but reading the passage in its context we begin to see how it relates to the presence of God in our conflicts of loyalty and truth.

Often in our dilemmas we are, consciously or not, looking for God in the situation. This is not a rarified spiritual exercise, but a practical search for an outside point of reference. That is what made the Bible so relevant in Nazi Germany. When all other points of reference were controlled in a totalitarian state, the experiences recounted in the Bible served as points of reference to decide what remained right or wrong.

However much it may be true that God searches for us, our response, our allowing ourselves to be found, is often a search for something which we might identify with God.

Meister Eckhart, the fourteenth-century mystic, who is always aware of the weakness of human nature because he

shares that weakness, points out that we need some
encouragement in our search for God:

> When one is looking for a thing and finds no trace of its
> existence one hunts half-heartedly and in distress. But
> lighting on some vestige of the quarry, the chase grows
> lively, blithe and keen. The man in quest of fire,
> cheered when he feels the heat, looks for its source with
> eagerness and pleasure. And so it is with those in quest
> of God: feeling none of the sweetness of God they grow
> listless but, sensing the sweetness of divinity, they
> blithely pursue their search for God.

It is the need for those vestiges of the thing we seek that
makes the Bible so powerful in its effect upon us. As we read
of some experience with God: Moses turning aside to see the
burning bush and having his whole vocation revealed – to
lead the Hebrew slaves out of Egypt; Peter blurting out the
answer to "Who do you say that I am?" and receiving his
commission to lead the Church; Paul on the Damascus
road, blinded and convicted by a vision of Jesus whom he
persecuted and discovering his destiny as the apostle to the
nations. Stand with these men for a while and you will not
investigate the burning bush, nor wonder if Peter was really
the rock on which the Church was founded, nor query the
reason for Paul's blindness; but you will find a vestige of
what you are looking for, you will sense the sweetness of God
and go on eagerly to search for his meaning in your own life.

The People who Wrote the New Testament
The New Testament is all about Jesus Christ, but he wrote
nothing that survives. Those who knew him were not very
good at writing either. They were so overwhelmed by the
experience of his presence, the power of the simple message

that he was raised from the dead by God, and the belief that he would soon come again to triumph over his enemies, that they had no time to write.

Saul of Tarsus, a fanatical Jew, who had received the best education his culture could provide, was shaken to the roots of his being by what he described as a resurrection appearance of Jesus on the Damascus road. He never knew Jesus of Nazareth, but he hated the effect of his teaching upon his fellow Jews. He harassed all who were converted to what he believed to be a new religion, a perversion of Judaism. It was on one of those fanatical quests that he came face to face with a vision of Jesus and was blinded by it for many days. Once he recovered his sight, he learnt all he could about Jesus from those who had known him, studied his teaching, and set out to explain it to Jews and Gentiles throughout the Ancient World which clustered around the Mediterranean and centred on Rome. Those who believed, he formed into churches, and kept in touch with them by correspondence and occasional visits – the letters he wrote were treasured, and some of them were collected and now form part of the New Testament.

The author of these letters was an educated Jew, who had embraced the Christian faith and brought his organizing power into it. He was able to think through the basic philosophy of the Christian Church, and respond to questions which troubled its believers. He was passionately concerned to see the Church opened up to the non-Jewish world. There is little doubt that the Church needed him at that time or it might have remained a sect of Judaism, limited to Palestine. His letters are urgent and topical, breathing the spirit of the untidy early Christian Church. The more we study the background of his life and relate his letters to the conflicts he had with his fellow Jews and his fellow Christians, the more it becomes obvious that he was a man of God's own choosing, raised up to spread the good news of the kingdom of God, to stir up the disciples to extend their view of the Church into all the world, and to clarify the meaning of what had happened in Jesus Christ. He gave the Church a theology, not static but dynamic, born of the conflicts in the churches to which he ministered. Much of the thinking today about the life, death and resurrection of Jesus comes from Paul's letters. And yet he hardly mentions any detail of the life of Jesus!

One of his companions was brought up as a Greek (i.e. a Gentile or non-Jew). He was called Luke, and there are all kinds of legends about him as a doctor (Paul's ''beloved physician'') and an artist (he is supposed to have painted the face of Mary, the mother of Jesus, through a mirror). He wrote more of the New Testament than any other single writer. First, his gospel, written apparently for a Greek convert called Theophilus. Then, for the same convert, he wrote the *Acts of the Apostles*, a very selective history of the first generation of Christians after the resurrection. It becomes a story of Paul mostly, and it is clear that Luke is an eye-witness of much of the later part of the book. We know very little about what Luke did, but it was providential to have on hand a man who could write so well at the crucial moments of the history of the expansion of the Christian Church. He was also a researcher and able to interview people who knew Jesus of Nazareth, witnesses of the resurrection appearances, as well as being able to read and edit such documents as Mark's gospel. His two writings come under the heading of ''written by one whom God raised up to write''. He saw something of Paul's ministry, to which he was able to witness. The readers, including Theophilus, who did not see the effect of Paul's ministry, are able to pay attention to one who was there.

We do not know for certain very much about the authors

of the other two gospels, Matthew and Mark. There was a John Mark who went with Paul and his mentor Barnabas on the first missionary journey, but who couldn't stand the pace, and turned back. Barnabas, to whom he appears to have been related, wanted to give the young man a second chance; but Paul thought he was not the stuff that missionaries are made of. They were, however, reconciled before the end of Paul's life. Tradition has it that this was the man who wrote the shortest and earliest gospel in the New Testament. There is a trivial story told towards the end of that gospel about a young man, to whom the story was not trivial, who was there the night Jesus was arrested and who rose from his sleep with only a sheet around him. When the guard saw him they ran after him and he fled naked. Such a story has no meaning in a gospel which is so economic with space unless it is a signature story, saying "I was there!"

Matthew's Gospel is a composite affair, but there is a very ancient tradition that part of it was from Matthew the disciple of Jesus. He is supposed to have collected the sayings of Jesus in their original Aramaic. Others translated them into Greek. Mark's Gospel provides the framework for Matthew, and other sources were used. Where the birth stories at the beginning came from no one knows, but they are different from Luke's. Some think the gospel was compiled for reading in the Christian synagogues, as it appears to reflect the life of the Church in its second generation.

The Fourth Gospel, which has the name of John attached to it, purports to be by a disciple, who is further described as "the disciple whom Jesus loved". At the end of the gospel there is an autobiographical note, commenting upon a rumour that Jesus had promised that this disciple would live to see his return, which implies a disciple who was very young, and who would outlive all the other disciples. The fourth Gospel is the writing of an old man who remembers. It needed to be different from the other three gospels, from which the historical facts were known, and passages from them, referred to as the "memoirs" of the apostles, were read in the Christian gatherings for worship. This old man wrote instead of the *meaning* of the gospels, proving in sermon form that Jesus was the Son of God and proclaiming the offer of eternal life. This was the gospel most needed at the end of the first century when the Church was already in decline.

Apart from a few short letters by authors other than Paul, but letters which served the same purpose, only one strange book remains.

We do not know who wrote "The Book of Revelation". Whoever he was, he wrote for a church in decline, forsaking its first love, losing its freshness. He wrote what he saw in an ecstatic vision of the future triumph of Christ and the end of the world. A declining and persecuted Church needed the lift which such a book could give. The author had a position of authority and leadership in the Church of his day, and wrote specifically to seven churches in Asia Minor, warning them against the loss or perversion of their faith. He was the man the Church needed at that time.

If we followed the authors of the books of the Old Testament in this same way, we should have great difficulty in locating some of them, but those we did would, like the authors of the books of the New Testament, qualify as those whom God had raised up at times of crisis to speak to his people. It is the urgent note which makes the Bible so compelling, and the sense of crisis which makes it strangely relevant in times when the Church is under threat – from without or within.

The Unrivalled Role of the Bible
We have seen that the authority of the Bible rests upon the

fact that at certain critical moments in the history of mankind, there were those who saw what God was doing in the world and bore witness to what they saw. This is as true of the Old as of the New Testament. No other writings have been so consistently used in "Christian" countries to mediate the will of God to men and women. It has no rival. The story of the translation of the Bible in every European country is one of epic struggles to make it available in the language of the people. The reason was the conviction that if a person sat down and read the Bible, aided or unaided, that person would sooner or later learn what God was saying to him through the words of the Bible; hence it was known as the Word of God. It is a confusing name because Christians believe that only Jesus Christ can properly be called the Word of God. The Bible has a unique role in communicating God's word to people. The reason for the confusion is obvious. Jesus was not only God's man, like a prophet, but he represented God, his life and teaching were mirrors of God. All our records of him are contained in the New Testament, and the Old Testament is the preparation for understanding his Gospel.

For centuries, the Bible was a secret treasure held by the priests, who alone had the grace to understand it. The simple people – what the learned Pharisees used to call "the people of the land who know not the law" – could learn from the priests or from wall paintings explained by the priest. When in the fourteenth century, John Wycliffe insisted that the simplest person should have access to the Bible he saw it as the Word of God open to all. The century or so which followed saw the struggle for the open Bible. It had its martyrs and its bigots, but at least in the lands of the Reformation, the Bible won through as the unique means of discovering the will of God. Those who could barely read turned to the Bible. Many who could not follow a theological

Living Christianity

argument, and found what sermons they did hear unintelligible, nourished themselves on Bible reading. No other book rivalled it for devotion. The story of the use of the Bible in England is an epic tale. The Psalms fanned revolution in Scotland and the Netherlands; the Old Testament provided the basis for law in England during the Commonwealth; the poor preachers with their Bibles broke the power of the priests as the Middle Ages crumbled.

From such an experience, the Bible developed an absolute authority. This did not serve the Church well when it came to conflicts with science or with historical research. Both the absolute authority of the Bible and the high regard of the people for it, resisted the reasonable criticism which should have been accepted to reveal new truth. But the Bible weathered even that to emerge as the basis of all Christian devotion, a guide to the Christian way of life and an authority which, if not based upon verbal inspiration, was in its own field supreme. As a moral guide it determined the ethics of a people. The decline of the churches, the destructive criticism of the Bible as distinct from the necessary analysis of its human origin, has led to the loss of any framework for a national morality. Even in its weakness, the Bible shows what once it meant to a people, and the difficulty of finding a substitute for it. The Bible can never again become the absolute authority that it was, but in the morality of a whole generation and the loss of a stable life style, we have learnt the danger of discrediting it.

The threefold cord - authors raised up by God, a consistent theme about God and his relationship with humankind, and its use - cannot easily be broken.

86

Chapter Six

WHO IS JESUS CHRIST FOR
US TODAY?

At the heart of Christianity is a figure in whom the believer will put his trust. He is a person who lived in a specific period of time and in a real place. His name as a village boy in Nazareth was Jesus, and he was the son of Mary. He had brothers and sisters and was brought up in a carpenter's family. It should not be difficult to reconstruct the kind of life he lived and the kind of person he was, but he appears to have puzzled people. Those who believed in him called him "the Christ". In Hebrew that would mean "the Messiah", but in the Greek-speaking world where faith in him grew, it had a much wider meaning. So when we set out to discover who he was, we have two searches: to discover all we can about a person who lived in first-century Galilee and made a name for himself as a preacher; and to discover what he meant to people who never knew him in his lifetime, but called him Jesus, the Christ, and who worshipped him and put their hopes for life and eternity in him. Both those who lived with him as a person in Galilee, and those who later put their trust in him, were part of a culture quite different from our own. They thought differently and expressed their experiences in different terms. This gives us a third search: what can we, in our culture today, make of this Jesus who was called Christ? That will be an important step towards discovering what Christianity is for us today.

The Quest of the Historical Jesus

It is clear from the last chapter that our only source for the life of Jesus is in the gospels. But it is impossible to get through the faith of the writers in Jesus as the Christ, the Son of God, to the plain portrait of the man. Albert Schweitzer surveyed the studies of Jesus from the eighteenth century to his own day, i.e. from Reimarus, a teacher of Oriental languages in Hamburg in the eighteenth century, to Wrede, a New Testament scholar at the end of the nineteenth century. In German, he called his book, *Von Reimarus zu Wrede*, but when it came into English it was called, *The Quest of the Historical Jesus*. John Bowden, in a very informative chapter of his book, *Jesus: The Unanswered Questions*, shows how unsuccessful Schweitzer was in his quest. He set out to find the historical Jesus, believing that when he had found him it would be possible to bring him straight into our time as teacher and saviour. But Schweitzer discovered that "those who went in search of the historical Jesus found not so much Jesus as themselves".

We may leave to one side for the moment the question as to whether that is perhaps the whole point of searching for Jesus – that we should find ourselves. Instead, let us first take two examples among many of people who have looked for the historic figure of Jesus of Nazareth in our time.

Nikos Kazantzakis, a Cretan writer, whose powerful style and imagination was demonstrated in the film version of his novel, *Zorba the Greek*, searched all his life for an authentic religion and a real Christ. In an early novel, *Christ Recrucified*, he explored the passion plays of Greece; in *Homage to Greco* he told of his journeys to the places of religious life in his country; but his first unambiguous attempt to look Jesus in the face was his controversial novel, *The Last Temptation*. His church excommunicated him. When, mistakenly I think, the novel was made into a film, he was vilified as a blasphemer. But his novel is a masterpiece, exploiting the full range of his imagination. He describes life around the Sea of Galilee with all the roughness of Cretan village life, and wrestles with a concept of Jesus which makes sense of his full humanity and the agony of carrying the burden of divinity. He turns traditional views of Jesus upside down. Here is no attractive, fair-haired and blue-eyed child, growing into the sweetness of youth. Jesus is a man possessed – and if, as believers say, he is truly God and truly man what else could he be? Kazantzakis feels the physical agony of reconciling the two natures in one person: the splitting head, the inexorable mission, the real temptations in the wilderness, the tension between the longings for a fully human life and the demands of a divine mission. He does not hesitate to show Jesus in love, or the attraction that he presented to women. His dream of family life comes to a climax in which he thinks of avoiding the cross, and depicts a meeting years later with Paul who is preaching about Christ. He denounces him and says – "No! It was not like that at all."

Kazantzakis is writing a novel, he knows his New Testament and he uses his knowledge of the harsh life of Crete to reconstruct the harsh life of Galilee. He also feels the human urges and will not deny them to Jesus. It is an outstanding example of a man coming to terms with the real problems of God's incarnation and its consequences in human society and human psychology. If Jesus was a man and if he really is the Son of God, then Kazantzakis' picture cannot be far from the truth. Unlike the historian or the biographer, he has not started with the life of a person, he has started with faith in a divine saviour and found the possibility of his being human intolerable. But if what Christians claim is true, then Kazantzakis has helped us to understand the price Jesus paid for what he did in agony and torment. The cross was not the worst; the worst was living with the contradictions in his own nature and the total misunderstanding of those who loved him.

Gerd Theissen, Professor of New Testament at Heidelberg, an imaginative writer and, of course, a reliable New Testament Scholar, has written a narrative study of Jesus of Nazareth called *The Shadow of the Galilean*. It is scrupulously written, taking into account even the most radical scholarship, presenting what could be taught at a university. He cuts no corners. But this is "narrative theology". When he had done his textual work, he wrote a narrative in which Jesus never appears – only his shadow, the influence he has upon others. It is clear that he was a disturbance. He transformed the tax office where Matthew worked, and changed the attitude of beggars to those who had money. Gamaliel is faced with his teaching about the Sabbath, and is troubled because it is not against the law, but Jesus has not thought through the consequences of his teaching. Even Barabbas has to think again about his mission of rebellion. What Gerd Theissen does is reconstruct what must have been the effect of Jesus if he said and did the things he is reported to have said and done in the gospels. And it turns the world upside down. One of the interesting methods employed in this book is to address a mythical German scholar at regular intervals, and argue for the accuracy of the assumptions in this narrative theology. The chief character in the book, who has searched for Jesus and found only his influence, at last sees him in the distance, dead on a cross. It leads to a frightening nightmare in which the beasts take over the world. In his dream he sees Jesus transformed:

> It was Jesus, a changed Jesus. I had only seen him once
> – from the city wall of Jerusalem. At that time he was

hanging dead on the cross, but now he radiated life, peace and freedom. The rule of the beasts was at an end. I woke up happy, but confused.

He goes into the open air and looks at the sea, and the light of dawn gradually washes away his fears. Never again would he wish the earth away. In him the rule of the beasts had come to an end. Jesus had given him back the earth. Then he prays and later comments:

> For a long time I stood like this on our house and let the dream of the man echo in me. The rule of the beasts could not last for ever. Some time the man had to appear, the true man. And everyone could recognize in him the features of Jesus.

Both these writers have used their imagination powerfully, they have added nothing to our knowledge of the historical Jesus, but both have in their own way been authentic and shown us that Jesus cannot be studied in quite the same way as Julius Caesar or Leonardo da Vinci. The gospel writers knew that, and therefore they discovered or invented a new literary style. It did not have to be accurate, but it had to be true. The four gospels do not deliberately falsify the historical material, but they present a figure which cannot be contained by the details of his life.

Presenting Jesus, the Christ, to an Alien Culture
The disciples had to explain to their fellow Jews that Jesus was more than meets the eye. He was not only an itinerant preacher, miracle worker and revolutionary who angered the authorities. He was the Christ, they said, and this caused trouble. However, they remained within the synagogues and they were not the only Jews who claimed that they followed a

teacher who was the promised Messiah. Among Jews, "Christ" meant "the Messiah". But what happened when you had to present Jesus the Christ to a non-Jewish people? At first, the movement away from their Jewish roots took them only to those who were called "God-fearers", not Jews but well instructed in the Jewish religion. The Acts of the Apostles contains a story which rings true about the baptism of one of these, an important man called Cornelius. The story tells of Peter being persuaded that he should go to the house of Cornelius. There the Holy Spirit came upon his household, just as it did at Pentecost, and Peter felt compelled to baptize them. Obviously this was revolutionary enough, and Peter was in trouble afterwards for doing it. But he never really moved outside the culture of Jewish religious ideas. The same was true of much of Paul's first missionary work. He took the Gospel to the Jews first and then to the Gentiles, who were, like Cornelius, mostly well informed about the Jewish religion.

The Acts of the Apostles tells of a strange episode in Athens. Paul was on his own, and he was looking around like a tourist at the great monuments of the intellectual centre of the ancient world. He was called upon to address a purely Gentile group who knew nothing of the Jewish religion or the promise of a Messiah. A group of Epicureans and Stoics began to argue with him. He was asked to explain his "strange ideas". The sermon or address which follows may not have been what he said, but it is recorded by Luke as such. And it is carved on stone in Athens in the original Greek. It is totally unlike any of the sermons Luke records as from Paul.

Usually, Paul falls back on his own conversion experience, but this time he does not. He has an audience who need to know first about God. Like a good speaker, he begins where his audience are. He points to their gods and singles out the altar "TO AN UNKNOWN GOD". He promises that he will tell them of this unknown God. He presents a clear outline of the Old Testament view of God, the sole Creator, who is a Spirit and does not live in temples. This God, he said, set men in their appropriate places in such a way that they "would seek him and perhaps reach out for him and find him". But of course they did not have far to search because God was within them. Paul even quotes one of their poets as having said as much. If God is within us, he should not be worshipped as an idol even of gold and silver; "an image made by man's design and skill" cannot be God. They are wrong to be idol worshippers, but God understands and does not punish them. At least, not yet! But his patience is coming to an end and he had appointed a time for judgement: "he has set a day when he will judge the world with justice by *the man he has appointed*". This is Paul's presentation of Jesus, the Christ, to a Gentile audience. They do not know of a Messiah. Christ for them means a cosmic Christ, the lord of all creation. This at least is the Christ Paul presents. They are still listening, because they understand him so far. The man God has appointed must be to them like some super-emperor, who will judge the world "with justice".

Paul then makes his mistake. From earliest times, the heart of the Christian message has been, "Christ is risen". To the inhabitants of Jerusalem a few weeks after the crucifixion, this made some sense and stir. They knew of Jesus, and many had seen and heard him. The disciples could with great effect say, "This Jesus whom you crucified" is risen – God raised him from the dead. Paul too had argued that the risen Jesus had appeared to him. But to this crowd in Athens, it made no sense. They had never heard of Jesus, and when Paul said, as evidence for his statement, that he was going to tell them of the unknown

God, and the man whom God had appointed, "He has given proof of this to all men by raising him from the dead", they laughed. Paul had presented the Christ to an alien culture quite effectively until he came to the resurrection.

The Power of a Crucified Christ

After Paul left Athens, where he did not stay to wait for his friends, he appears to have gone in depression to Corinth. He returned to his trade and stayed with some Christian family who gradually nursed him back to faith. He began preaching again in Corinth. It was different now. In the synagogue he had no difficulty, but he now faced a Gentile audience also, and knew that the cutting edge of his message was not the resurrection. He did not risk the same results as at Athens. Some years after, in one of his letters to Corinth, he himself describes what he preached. It was not with eloquence, he says, nor any superior wisdom, no triumphalism: "For I resolved to know nothing while I was with you except Jesus Christ and him crucified." This does not mean that he ceased to believe in the resurrection. In that same letter, he lists the resurrection appearances and proves the truth of the resurrection. But on his first visit to Corinth after the failure in Athens, he presented a crucified Christ to a gentile audience. It was paradoxical preaching. He knew what an offence this would be to the Jews. The idea of a crucified Messiah meant a Messiah, God's Messiah, who had failed. There were, of course, many Messiahs who failed in those turbulent days, but because they failed they were deemed false Messiahs. The only answer to that in the first generation of Christians had been, "This Jesus, whom you crucified, God hath made both Lord and Christ". To the Gentiles, who had no tradition of Messiahs, the word "Christ" meant conqueror. And to present a crucified Christ was sheer foolishness. Paul discovered, however, that

if he preached a crucified Christ it had power to change
men's lives. It was not the life of Jesus, but the way he
accepted death for others that made the most powerful
appeal. Paul had no consistent theory of how it happened,
but he saw men set free from bondage, able to throw off a
lifetime of guilt, liberated because in Jesus abandoned they
discovered their worth: "He did this for me." Paul had in
fact abandoned all attempts to be clever. He saw that there
was a foolishness in God, that Jesus was God's clown. What
others called foolishness, he discovered to be the simplicity of
God. God, the Father, does not sit waiting for us to come
and repent. In Christ, he comes into our world and appeals
to us. He reconciles rebel humanity to himself. If that sounds
a bit metaphysical, listen to how Paul arrives at his
astonishing conclusion.

The church at Corinth was proud of its intelligent
members. They could speculate and philosophize like the
Stoics and Epicureans he met in Athens. He knew them for
what they were. Yet they were Christians, his own converts
and he reasoned with them:

> God sent me to you to preach the Gosel – not with words
> of human wisdom, lest the cross of Christ be emptied of
> its power.

All right, he continues, I know that a crucified Christ makes
nonsense. It is foolishness. "But to us who are being saved it
is the power of God." The God who raised Jesus from the
dead might inspire confidence, but what was it more than all
the mythology of Greece with gods doing wonders? Even the
Jews would put one miracle against another and say that
Moses did greater miracles. Certainly, the resurrection
would win neither Jew nor Greek. Jesus is reported to have
said, in one of his memorable parables: "Though one should

rise from the dead they will not believe.'' God who has acted for the salvation (i.e. the healing and the liberation) of mankind has bypassed human wisdom:

> Where is the wise man? Where is the scholar? Where is the philosopher of this age? Has not God made foolish the wisdom of the world? For since in the wisdom of God the world through its wisdom did not know him, God was pleased through the foolishness of what was preached to save those who believe.

He knew his fellow Jews and how they lusted after miracles. It was reported that they had demanded a special miracle from Jesus and he had refused to give it to them. The new Paul faced both Jew and Greek with the cross. He knew that it was a stumbling block to Jews and foolishness to Greeks, but he persisted because he now saw that Christianity was not intended to be a miracle-working religion, nor was it a philosophy. Later, the Christian apologists would try to reconcile Christianity with the best in Greek philosophy, and later still, under the Christian emperor, they would try to make it a religion of power. Both were false. Paul had detected a characteristic of Christ that we can never ignore. He did not present him as a conqueror, nor as the founder of a new philosophy or ideology; but as vulnerable. The taunts of his enemies as recorded in the gospels have an element of truth in them – ''He saved others; himself he could not save.'' We are back with that middle stanza in Bonhoeffer's poem, quoted in the Introduction:

> Men go to God when he is sore bestead,
> Find him poor and scorned, without shelter or bread,
> Whelmed under weight of the wicked, the weak, the dead;
> Christians stand by God in his hour of grieving.

That is the consequence of Paul's presentation of Christ to an alien culture. But he soon discovers that it is the presentation he must make to the Jews also. Once we face the problem of how to present Christ to a different culture, we learn something new about him. Our own struggle to present Christ to our secularized, post-Christian culture, is not only a problem in communication, but also a voyage of discovery. Only when we struggle with the question, ''Who is Jesus Christ for us today?'', do we discover who Jesus Christ is. We do not have a solid body of facts which need interpreting, but a person whom we are learning to know as we discover how to present him to an alien culture. Every missionary knows this or fails.

When I was still in my teens. I was much impressed by the books of Stanley Jones, whose titles were of the form *The Christ of the Indian Road*, or *the Chinese Road*. He maintained that not until we have seen Christ on the road of every culture have we truly known him. But it is not always gain. Some attempts to adapt the Gospel to a culture have resulted in the loss of Christ. This was true of the age of Constantine, as Jerome constantly bemoans. The attractions of a culture can take away the offence of the Gospel, and this Paul avoided – except briefly on Mars Hill in Athens.

The Christ of Deprivation and Poverty

There is an extended parable recorded in Matthew's Gospel which is in the style of a prophecy, as though Jesus is describing what will happen at the Last Judgement. It recalls Paul's ''he hath set a day when he will judge the world with justice by the man he has appointed''. The gospel describes Christ coming into power to judge the nations, and he separates them as a shepherd separates sheep and goats. Then the point of the parable becomes the criteria of judgement. The sheep are those who have cared for those in need; the goats are those who did not bother. Both are surprised, and Jesus explains the reason for these criteria. They were serving or not serving him – for he was incognito in those who needed help: the hungry, the thirsty, the strangers, the ill clad, the sick and those in prison. That is where Christ is to be found. Russian literature is full of those who sought God, and did not recognize him because he came in the disguise of a beggar.

This means more than supporting Christian Aid. It means participating in the suffering of humanity as Christ did in his human life as Jesus of Nazareth. To be a believer means to participate in the movement of love which brought Christ to share our human life, emptying himself of his power and glory, and assuming the fragility, the temptation and, could one say, even the guilt of man, giving his own life unto death on the cross.

Paul waxes lyrical when he describes that in a Letter to the church at Philippi! This is a great deal more than imitation. The believer does not only proclaim Christ by doing the kind of things that he would do. Paul has one other saying which helps us to see the difference. It is put in context by, an Argentinian theologian, an active Methodist pastor, who has not hesitated to participate in the struggle for justice in his country, even co-operating with Marxists: a liberation theologian. His book on *Christians and Marxists* appeared in 1976, and in a passage which tries to show the particular Christian role in the struggle for human rights he says:

> What is here at stake is not mere imitation, but participation in the solidarity of love, the only thing that can create the possibility of new life for man. For this reason the Apostle Paul does not hesitate in

referring to his own suffering – physical as well as spiritual – as his participation in "what still has to be fulfilled of the sufferings of Christ". It is not that Christ left something undone, but that he opened for us a way of serving men in which the disciple enters now, paying the price, or as Jesus himself said, taking up his cross.

As we read through Paul's letters, we do not, as some have said, find that he has changed the teaching of the Church, but that he has discovered who Christ is for his generation and the cultures which he met in the Gentile world. We have now to take that one step further and ask, "Who is Jesus Christ *for us today?*"

The Ups and Downs of Church History
Unlike science, theology does not get better, meaning that the latest is the best. No one would try to learn his science from an old text book, because the new discoveries and new developments of thought will have provided more accurate conclusions than the writer of the old book could possibly know. Theology is not like that, and when we ask, "Who is Jesus Christ?", we tend to go in the opposite direction and say the oldest is best. But neither is always true. The attempts by Paul to break away from the limited Jewish image of Christ enlarged his and our understanding. But it did not go on like that. Already in the New Testament there are myths and theories spun that confuse our image of Christ, and once church doctrine became formalized it became more difficult to have any clear vision of a contemporary Christ. He was cast in an orthodox form, and the more speculative thinkers gained new insights, the more rigid became the orthodox formulae. It is well nigh impossible to find a living Christ in the Nicene Creed.

Once orthodoxy has the power to enforce its views, new light is shut off. Constantine wanted a uniform Church to support a uniform empire, and he was in no mood to tolerate individual opinions. The inheritance of Constantine cast its long shadow over the Middle Ages, and Christ became the merchandise of a priestly class. Nothing angered John Wycliffe more in the fourteenth century than the power which the priests had over the people, because they could dispense salvation, giving or withholding the body of Christ. Wycliffe was the Morning Star of the Reformation, and only after a very bitter struggle did the freedom to meet Christ in the Scriptures become available to all. Even then, the freedom was limited. Catholic and Protestant alike enforced their teaching upon their subjects. There was some freedom among the intellectuals, but right up to the nineteenth century, the Church taught that Christ was known and defined according to orthodox understanding.

It is only with the decline of the churches' authority that new insights have flourished. Some of these are a bit wild and unhelpful, but not all. In the last section we began to see how the liberation theologians in South America were beginning to find much of Paul's writing relevant. It was not taken over uncritically, but adapted and selected. Some of the things that Paul wrote are totally irrelevant to our way of living and thinking today. Some of the corrections to his teaching which emerged in the Middle Ages are found to be relevant. There is obviously a great deal of important material in the New Testament, without which we could know nothing of Jesus, and very little of the impact of Christ on the first generation of Christians. There is also some value in studying the history of the Church and noting the experience that many generations have had of the living Christ and how they have lived as a result. The Bible and Tradition – these are two elements in our search for Jesus

Christ, and we must take them seriously. But we have to do our own searching in our own generation.

For Us Today

Armed with a reasonable assessment of the Bible and Tradition, we must make two journeys – into ourselves and into our world. That is an inward search to the depth of our being, and an outward search to confront our world as it is. It may be that we want to change the world, but we must first begin by accepting it. A Jesus Christ totally unrelated to the modern world is a museum specimen. Again, we may not like the depth of our being, we may know that what we are going to find there is as unpleasant as Freud's unconscious. A Jesus Christ who is shocked by the depth of our being is not our saviour.

First then, our journey out into the world. Religion is too often secluded, as though we could only meet with God when we are cut off from the world. We even use the term "otherworldly" for a religious experience. Rabindranath Tagore, the Bengali poet, offers a rebuking word:

> Leave this chanting and singing and telling of beads!
> Whom dost thou worship in this lonely dark corner of a
>   temple with doors all shut?
> Open thine eyes and see thy God is not before thee!

Tagore led his worshipper out into the hard life of village India. We go out into a much more pleasant world. Science has made it comfortable for us – running water, hot and cold; electric light; refrigerators; washing machines; computers; our own home; enough to eat; transport, perhaps our own car; holidays in exotic places. Almost everybody in Britain is living a life more comfortable because science has developed and put much at our service.

The cities are no longer dark, but they are still violent. We have many more possessions than our grandfathers and grandmothers had, but we are vulnerable to burglars. We have better wages, but there is the hatred of industrial disputes. We are able to produce food in plenty to feed the world; but we do not distribute it to all. We are not in want, but others have more than we do, and that creates a longing. Success brings stress. We give our family more and the divorce rate rises, while our children find relief from boredom in drugs. We have a democratic system and just laws; but there are many in our society who suffer privation and poverty, homeless and unemployed. We are generous, raising large sums of money to feed the starving in Africa; but we are unable to solve the problems of injustice in our own cities or contain the hatred of the poor for the rich. We have a divided society of privilege and deprivation, with little desire on either side to bridge the gap. We could go on with this polarized society.

Who is Jesus Christ in all this greedy, materialistic society, which seems to be made up of quite nice people when you know them one by one? He oversimplifies! He says that you need no other commandment than "Love one another". That is sensible enough in a small, closely knit society like his group of disciples. But how can it work in a complex modern society? Sydney Carter in his song, "The Lord of the Dance", has portrayed Jesus Christ as the leader of a human dance. Stephen Verney in his book *The Dance of Love* has taken up this figure and developed it. He attempts to bring new life back into the great religious words like "glory" and "repentance"; but he also portrays Christian activity in Liverpool as a dance led by two bishops:

> In Liverpool today, which outsiders see only as a city of riots and of litter in the streets, but where insiders say,

"I wouldn't live anywhere else", the Roman Catholic Archbishop and the Anglican Bishop are, as it were, leading the dance together, and inviting everybody to join in. This is more influential than any number of sermons, because it points us towards a vision of glory which alone has power to transform our human egocentricity, and to bring us to a new way of seeing things which makes possible a new way of doing things.

And when you read *Better Together* by the bishop and the archbishop, and learn of this Christian partnership in a hurt city, you cannot fail to see that Jesus Christ is there, leading the dance of love. It is in fact easier to see him in that hurt city than it is among the Yuppies of the City, although surely he grieves there too and is not irrelevant.

The other journey must be to the depth of our being. We are indeed complex creatures, all of us, and few know what is really going on inside the other. Lovers may explore the body and feel a sense of intimacy, but there is often a wall separating those who "make love". We are as incapable of penetrating the inner life of the other as we are of facing up honestly to our own. Many of the stories told in the Fourth Gospel (John) are of the way in which Jesus penetrated the inner thoughts of the people he met – a Samaritan woman by the well, a man born blind, a woman taken in adultery and condemned to death for it, a sorrowing sister at the grave of her brother. What Jesus did in all these cases is less striking than how he related. In describing a controversy with the religious leaders, the Evangelist comments of Jesus that many people believed in him, but Jesus did not entrust himself to them, "for he knew all men", and then in the next verse adds, "he knew what was in a man". In our search for ourselves we need this Jesus. He is not a psychiatrist helping us to face up to what is buried in our unconscious, but one who knows us in our innermost thoughts.

Jean Vanier, in his work among mentally disabled people, has found that same penetration. He has often said, "I went to help them, but I have learnt far more from them than they have from me". His movement is in many countries – *L'Arche* it is called in France, The Ark. The experience is repeated again and again. Looking into the face of a man or woman whose mind is not fully under control or not developed in the way we measure sanity, you can see something more than the person you thought you knew. The words of Jesus are often proved true – "inasmuch as you did it to the least of these, you did it unto me". Look closely, you will see the face of Jesus, and he will understand what is in you.

Our journey into ourselves ultimately becomes our journey with someone else, and very often it is with one who is suffering or deprived. We discover our inner selves in solidarity with suffering humanity – it is participating in the cross again.

We cannot describe who Jesus Christ is for us today, but we can meet him. Once we have met him our values change, and we see ourselves in a different light. When Matthew records that Jesus sent his disciples out into all the world, to teach all nations, or to make disciples of all nations, the burden of their message was repentance. We must take the harshness out of that word. As Jesus used it and as his disciples understood it, it had nothing to do with punishment. It was merely a change of heart and mind. It meant letting go of preconceived ideas of God learnt from others and accepting the loving relationship of God as Father, which makes us kin to all humankind.

Chapter Seven

THE WAYWARDNESS OF THE
HOLY SPIRIT

There is self-evidently some difficulty in relating to a person who lived two thousand years ago. The major problem is making the connection, and historical research does not give us much to go on with Jesus of Nazareth. The effect he had upon those who knew him gives us more material, and what we know of his teaching gives us some guide for living and the acceptance of values. We have seen that we use our imagination on this material, we tend to discover ourselves. This is not a negative result because it enables us to participate with him in the suffering of humanity. But how do we make the connection?

Traditionally, the Church has done this by one of the vaguest of its doctrines – that of the Holy Spirit. Like so many doctrines intended to explain and make clear for ordinary Christians, this has led to a hardening and a rigid formula where it is least appropriate. It has landed us with the doctrine of the Trinity, which explains nothing. All New Testament references to this doctrine of God the Father, Son and Holy Ghost, not three gods, but One, are suspect as later additions. Most of the New Testament has no tidy doctrine of the Holy Spirit at all. Luke gives the impression that the Holy Spirit took hold of the disciples on the Day of Pentecost, and enabled them to make sense of a confusing situation, and to gain confidence in what they had to say about Jesus. The Fourth Gospel portrays the Holy Spirit as one who would come after the death of Jesus, and help the disciples to remember and understand what Jesus had taught them. It is in this Fourth Gospel that we get the corrective to any attempt to pin down the Holy Spirit and define what he or she or it is like or liable to do.

> The wind blows wherever it pleases. You hear its sound, but you cannot tell where it comes from or where it is going. So it is with everyone born of the spirit.

That occurs in a passage in which Jesus is portrayed as discussing with Nicodemus, a member of the Jewish ruling council, the need to be reborn. The concept strikes Nicodemus as very odd. Jesus says, "unless a man is born again [or it could be 'born from above'], he cannot see the kingdom of God." When Nicodemus rejects the whole idea Jesus adds "unless a man is born of water and the Spirit he cannot enter the kingdom of God". It is the person who is "born again" or "born of the Spirit" who is as unpredictable and inexplicable as the wind. Today, we would perhaps say, as a hurricane – we see its devastation, but are never quite sure how it stirs up such power and why it blows itself out. It is very difficult to fit that eruption into our lives with a doctrine of the Trinity. Artists and poets have tried to depict a more dynamic Trinity. Stephen Verney has drawn upon the icons to talk of a dance of love between Father, Son and Holy Spirit. It is not an easy doctrine to live with, and the Church has been very foolish to condemn those who found it difficult to believe.

The Ancestry of the Spirit

The Holy Spirit was not invented by the Christians. She is evident throughout the Old Testament too. In the very first chapter of Genesis, when the earth was formless and empty, darkness covering the deep, ''the Spirit of God was hovering over the waters''. She is like a bird, brooding over her eggs until they come to birth. All that is mythical and therefore profound. Creation is at the heart of Judaeo-Christian thought, and every explanation is of necessity a myth. In the Book of Proverbs there is a delightful picture of ''Wisdom'', who takes the place of ''Spirit'', and like a daughter delights and plays before her father, who is creating the world. She feels herself to be the master craftsman:

> The Lord brought me forth at the beginning of his work,
> before his deeds of old;
> I was appointed from eternity,
> from the beginning before the world began.
> When there were no oceans, I was given birth,
> when there were no springs abounding with water;
> before the mountains settled in place,
> before the hills I was given birth,
> before he made the earth or its fields
> or any of the dust of the world.
> I was there when he set the heavens in place,
> when he marked out the horizon on the face of the deep,
> when he established the clouds above
> and fixed securely the fountains of the deep,
> when he gave the sea its boundary
> so that the waters could not overstep his command,
> and when he marked out the foundations of the earth.
> Then I was the craftsman at his side.
> I was filled with delight day by day,
> rejoicing always in his presence,
> rejoicing in his whole world
> and delighting in mankind.

The picture of a daughter delighting in her father's creation is a very beautiful one.

But the Spirit also occurs in other contexts in the Old Testament. It is the Spirit of God who moves the Prophets so that they are capable of doing what they could never accomplish alone. "I will put my Spirit upon him" or "within you". In the old stories of Saul, the first Hebrew king, there is one in which he joined with a band of charismatic "prophets". As he dances with them in ecstasy, the people exclaim in surprise, "Is Saul also among the prophets!" But more usually in the Old Testament, "the Spirit of God came upon him with power", or as discernment, enabling a person to understand. It is basically the communication of the wisdom, or the will or the power of God, however the Spirit is manifest.

The Baptism of Jesus

There is no reason to doubt the fact that Jesus was baptized by John the Baptist. The disciples, many of whom had been followers also of John the Baptist, have to explain why Jesus was baptized. John was calling for repentance, which apart from turning one's back on a sinful life, meant getting one's relationship with God right. If all they said about Jesus was true – God's Messiah, the Christ, the Son of the Living God, destined to share power with God the Father Himself – how come that he needed to be baptized? They insisted that it was a choice made by Jesus and that John agreed reluctantly. It certainly was an act of approval for John's ministry. But what happened when he was baptized? The gospels say two things about this baptism – the Spirit descended upon him and the Spirit drove him into the wilderness of temptation. The Spirit of God was the authenticator of who Jesus really was, and his guide through life. When he comes to the synagogue at Nazareth, he takes as his own the words from the Book of Isaiah, "The Spirit of the Lord God is upon me". Later, when they accused him of being in league with the devils, he claimed that he cast out devils by the Spirit of God.

John the Baptist is also reported as saying that his own baptism was only a preliminary. He pointed to another, whom he is said to have identified with Jesus in many different ways, as the One who should come – and this One would baptize with the Spirit. Again, the Spirit is the means of communication of God's grace and God's power.

The Fourth Gospel

It is in "John" that we have the most extended teaching about the Holy Spirit. Like Socrates, it is in the form of a conversation with his disciples. As the gospel is written in Greek, the word *pneuma* is used. Like the Hebrew word *Ruah*, it means wind (pneumatic tyres come from this root!) There is something quite primitive in this idea of a spirit like the wind. Early man must have noted the force and movement of the wind, and thought of it as a kind of spirit inhabiting nature, as the breath inhabits man, like a soul. The two words *Ruah* and *pneuma* were much alike although with subtle differences. In the Fourth Gospel they act and react upon one another. Christians took the word "Spirit" and added the adjective "Holy". They were thus taking a general idea of "spirit" and using it to interpret the continuing relationship with God which they were aware of after the end of the physical life of Jesus. Occasionally they would talk of the "the spirit of Jesus", and they had other names long before the Holy Spirit was given the same rank as the Father and the Son. There is an interesting dispute between the churches of the East and West which centuries later left a memory of the confusion. The East with its subtle language had defined the Trinity and gave equal weight to each of the three persons. At the first Ecumenical Council in Nicea in 325, they affirmed that the Son was of the same substance with the Father, and later tidied up the equation by giving the Holy Spirit an equal rank. Then, when the Roman Church moved into dominance and Latin became the language of the Western Empire, the clumsy Latin language could hardly bear the subtleties of Greek disputes and defined the Spirit as coming *from* the Father and the Son, which undoubtedly gave the Son a rank above the Spirit. East and West split over that *filioque* (i.e. "and the Son") clause. In such disputes and doctrinal statements the whole freshness of the Spirit was lost in arguments over abstractions.

The Fourth Gospel has none of this. There, in the Socratic dialogue with Jesus helping his disciples to face the inevitable separation, he assures them that he is only going away for "a little while", and that in fact his going away is something that they should welcome because what takes his place is better. It is important that we recognize that these dialogues were not recorded interviews. Jesus probably never spoke like this, but it is how a later generation explained what he meant when he comforted the disciples before his inevitable death. They were obviously devastated by the idea that he would die and that they would be left alone. The Fourth Gospel tells of Peter vowing that he wants to die with Jesus. He is told that he will die in due time and will follow Jesus after death, and that sets off the dialogue. We shall look only at those parts in the three long chapters that deal with the promise of the Holy Spirit, under various names.

Another Counsellor

Jesus gives the disciples some instructions about how they are to live, and answers their questions about his continuing existence, close to the Father. Then he adds:

"I will ask the Father, and he will give you another Counsellor to be with you for ever."

Clearly this is to be someone who will replace Jesus as their spiritual guide. The word "counsellor" is a difficult one and has been variously translated – the old use of the word "comforter" was quite good, when it still had the original meaning of standing by one's side and supporting (*com* = with; *fort* = strong). But a definition is given at once in the text – "the Spirit of Truth". This Spirit is understood in the language and thought of the first century, as within those who believe, but rejected by those who do not. The Fourth Gospel describes those who are opposed to the young Christian Church as "the world". The world cannot accept this Spirit of Truth, because she is a continuance of the presence of Jesus – now "within" the believers and living with them. It is an exact parallel to the relationship they had with Jesus when he was physically with them. Now after his death and resurrection, they have a relationship which is deeper. The Spirit of Truth enables the relationship to continue at a deeper level. The description of this is poetic:

Before long, the world will not see me any more, but you will see me. Because I live, you also will live.

That is the first function of the Spirit – to continue the relationship. Every bereaved person will understand. What is most desired when a loved one dies is to retain the old relationship. The imagination – and remember Shakespeare's perceptive lines:

lunatics, lovers, and poets are of imagination all compact –

often enables a bereaved person to meet the beloved after death, in dreams, visions and fantasies. The fulfilment of this longing is promised here and, because the text is written generations later, has already been experienced.

It is Judas (not Iscariot) who asks the question about "the world". Why does Jesus limit this promise to the disciples? He is told that it is not so limited. The words in the text are:

> If anyone loves me, he will obey my teaching. My Father will love him, and we will come to him and make our home with him.

In this gospel, we read the conviction of the Church of that period that Jesus came, not for an elect few, but for all who could believe. God's love was for the whole world:

> For God so loved the world that he gave his one and only Son, that whoever believes in him shall not perish but have eternal life.

The universal love and universal appeal was strongly emphasized by the Church at the end of the first century, even though they were a tiny minority in a mighty empire. The Spirit of Truth is not only for the disciples, but for all who believe and live according to the teaching of Jesus. To all these, the other counsellor is promised.

The Functions of the Spirit of Truth

Apart from being a communication with the Jesus who lived as a man on earth, the Spirit of Truth is to have specific functions in the life of the believer. At this point, the Counsellor, already referred to as the Spirit of Truth, is also identified as the Holy Spirit, who "will teach you all things and will remind you of everything I have said to you".

For the disciples that is quite simple. The Holy Spirit will keep their memory fresh, and even those things which they did not understand at the time will come back to them with new meaning. In this way, by the help of God's Holy Spirit, sent by God to them, they will be able to live according to the teaching of Jesus. But to a subsequent generation, for whom this gospel was written and therefore also for us, it means that God will provide an inspiration by which we can, if we will, understand the teaching of Jesus and live according to it. There is assurance in that. We do not have to live in fear and anxiety, lest we have got it wrong. The sincere believer can be at peace, without fear, because the Spirit of Truth will lead him into all truth. That makes sense, not because it is written down as the supposed words of Jesus to his disciples, but because those who believe in him and have any sense of the awareness of God are at peace in the knowledge that God loves them. It is not a religion of rules that must not be broken, but a relationship which is secure.

The following chapter in the Fourth Gospel uses the figure of the vine, comparing Jesus with a vine and God as the vine dresser. Those who believe are like fruitful branches of the vine. The branches are pruned by a loving God. That which is cut away is that which is preventing growth – and it is destroyed. The Holy Spirit is then the fructifying sap which flows from Jesus the Christ into his followers. The pruning is not punishment for the violation of laws, but for the purpose of growth and fruitfulness. An image must not be pushed too far, but this is a very useful one. It is of course a later interpretation to assume that the branches cut off are those who refuse to believe. They are rather those things hindering our growth. The disciplining of the vine allows the sap to flow.

The lesson drawn from the vine parable is that our relationship to Christ is not that of inferiors, but of friends.

There is a love between us, comparable with the love of God, who prunes us that we may bear more fruit. There the command to all believers remains one and single, **"Love one another"**. No other commandment is necessary.

The disciples are warned that the world is not generally run on the principle of love, and therefore followers of Jesus may well be hated for the rebuke their lives present to a loveless world. They will suffer, as in fact Jesus suffered. The warning spelt out in the Fourth Gospel was with hindsight. The Church had by then known the fires of persecution. In a way the warning is an explanation of why the Church was so unpopular. We do not need to go back to the first century to learn that love is greeted with derision if not hatred in a world devoted to profit and greed.

At this point, another function of the Holy Spirit emerges. She is to testify to the truth of Jesus the Christ and his teaching, also to enable his followers to testify, giving them confidence and the appropriate words to speak.

This is followed by a section on "The Work of the Holy Spirit", spelt out in detail. It begins with the statement, which must have seemed unbearably untrue to the disciples, but less difficult for us:

It is for your good that I am going away.

The meaning becomes evident as the text continues. A new relationship with Jesus is necessary for full development. The rabbi/disciple relationship was that of childhood. The disciple must mature, become the Christ himself or herself. Through believers, the message of Jesus will reach the whole world, and successive generations will have to meet new problems. It will not be enough to go back constantly to the teaching of the most wonderful teacher who ever lived, in the limited understanding of the first century in Palestine. The teaching of Jesus must be enlarged and adapted to successive situations. The human race matures, makes new discoveries, understands the world better, takes more responsibility for the problems of living in a more and more complex world, etc. As believers we should welcome this growth and these changes – a growth for humanity towards autonomy. Then, in a way that a first-century Jew could not do, the Spirit of Truth can "guide you into all truth". The truth is the truth of God, and as we face new worlds, it is with excitement that we see the development of the human race and understand the revelation of God in human achievement. As believers live in the world, they do not try to get it back to the world of the first century, so that the sayings of Jesus might be relevant there. Instead they discover new truths in God at work in new worlds. There is not one set of truths delivered once and for all to the saints. Rather, those who "are born of the Spirit" are unpredictable, like the wind. The Fourth Gospel even makes Jesus say of all he had done, "Greater things than these shall you do because I go to my Father", and the Holy Spirit comes to you.

And his final admonition to a persecuted Church, or a bewildered people, "Take heart! I have overcome the world".

(This section is taken from John 14-16)

The Charismatic Movement
The waywardness of the Holy Spirit is illustrated by the analogy of the wind, or, as I have suggested, the hurricane! This is taken up by a number of groups among the Christian churches, which we conveniently lump together as the charismatic movement. That movement seeks to remind us all that there are specific "spiritual gifts", or *charismata*. Traditionally, these gifts are healing, speaking with tongues, ecstatic preaching and praying. Such observable phenomena

are usually accompanied by an intense sense of fellowship. The commandment to love one another is accepted and lived. The movement stretches across all denominations, and there are charismatics among Catholics as well as independent Pentecostal churches. These spiritual gifts go back to the earliest days of the Church and have broken out in different periods of its history. They cannot be denied as gifts of the Holy Spirit, and when they are allowed to enrich the fellowship of believers and serve the world in self-sacrificing work, sharing with Christ in the suffering of humanity, they are powerful. But there are charismatic movements which are divisive and show little sign of love outside the intimate communion of their own type.

Paul had problems with this defective type of spiritual gift and too narrow interpretation. The most damaging tendency is to regard Christians who do not manifest these unusual signs as being not fully Christian. There is no New Testament justification for such excluding claims for the gifts of the Holy Spirit – in fact the contrary. We are once again led back to the First Letter of Paul to the Corinthians – a most illuminating letter. No less than three chapters in that letter are devoted to spiritual gifts.

Paul and the Corinthian Christians
The Corinthians were obviously confused about spiritual gifts. They had members who spoke with tongues and thought themselves spiritually superior to those who did not. In the previous chapter, Paul had to take them to task for shocking behaviour at the Communion Service, and he implied a very distinct lack of love among them. Then he instructed them about spiritual gifts. Most of them had come from paganism and had very curious ideas of magic. He had patiently to explain that gifts of the Spirit are of many different kinds, but all such genuine gifts are for the common

good – that is the test, not individual pride. He listed the
kind of gifts to expect and carefully chose the order:
"wisdom, knowledge, faith, healing, miraculous powers,
prophecy, ability to distinguish between spirits, speaking in
tongues, interpretation of tongues." The important thing is
to recognize that there are no special grades. They are all
from the one Spirit, who "gives to each man, just as he
determines".

These various gifts are like the various members of the
body. They need each other. It is as though the whole
Church were the body of Christ and each individual like a
member of it. Again, Paul begins to list the kind of people
that make up the body of Christ and enable it to work:

> God has appointed in the church, first of all apostles
> [these were the disciples who had been sent out to
> proclaim the kingdom], second prophets, third
> teachers, then workers of miracles, also those having
> gifts of healing, those able to help others, those with
> gifts of administration, and those speaking in different
> kinds of tongues.

It is not necessary for everybody to have all the gifts, Paul
says. We get some pictures of that strange church in Corinth
from that list. It is not an unalterable list by any means.
Writing to other churches he had a different one. And if
today you visited a church in deprived urban areas or in the
isolated rural areas or in some country where another
religion predominates, you would find quite different lists.
Whatever is needed in the situation, that which unaided we
could not do, but need to do, someone is found who has the
required gift of the Spirit. She breathes life into human
communities in their need, and they don't all have to be
churches. Think of doctors, nurses, community workers in

the Lebanon of today. Whether they are consciously Christian or not, the Spirit breathes and the unexpected happens.

Paul was speaking to a Christian community, and because he found that they had their priorities wrong and lusted after spectacular gifts, he showed to them the greatest gift of all – love. His chapter on that theme is now a classic, but it must be the climax to this section because it perfectly expresses the priorities of the Spirit:

> If I speak in the tongues of men and of angels, but have not love, I am a resounding gong and a clanging cymbal.
>
> If I have the gift of prophecy and can fathom all mysteries and all knowledge, and if I have a faith that can move mountains, but have not love I am nothing.
>
> If I give all I possess to the poor and surrender my body to the flames, but have not love, I gain nothing.
>
> Love is patient, love is kind. It does not envy, it does not boast, it is not proud. It is not rude, it is not self-seeking, it is not easily angered, it keeps no record of wrongs. Love does not delight in evil but rejoices with the truth. It always protects, always trusts, always hopes, always perseveres.
>
> Love never fails. But where there are prophecies, they will cease; where there are tongues, they will be stilled; where there is knowledge, it will pass away.

When we talk of being born again, or being baptized by the Spirit, we are not talking of some exotic or ecstatic experience, but of a realization that this is the way we live in the Spirit. And of course we fail, as the disciples failed Jesus, but we come back never forsaking the vision. The Spirit does not fail us and she is always there to heal.

Unexpectedly you will find the work of the Spirit, and you will not know where it comes from or whither it is bound. Like the hurricane it will leave its mark behind. Unlike the hurricane, she is not destructive but life-giving. There is a story in the Book of Ezekiel in the Old Testament which prepares the way for the Christian view of the life-giving Holy Spirit, who alone has preserved the Church as a living witness to Jesus Christ, rather than a fossil of an earlier age.

The Valley of Dry Bones

Ezekiel 37 finds a weary and dispirited prophet whom the Spirit of God had brought to a valley which has been the scene of a battle. The glory of Israel's army had been slain. In a vision, the prophet sees the dry bones and God asks him, "Can these bones live?" He throws the question back to God. Eventually he is used by God to provoke the *Ruah* (breath, wind, spirit) to blow through the valley, and the bodies of the soldiers come together, tendon upon tendon. The *Ruah* blows again and they come alive and stand on their feet – a mighty army! It is a vision and the interpretation is given:

> These bones are the whole house of Israel. They say, "Our bones are dried up and our hope is gone; we are cut off ",

To which God responds:

> "I will put my Spirit in you and you will live."

The vision and the parallel to the dying Church of our day is obvious.

Chapter Eight

WORSHIP IN A SECULAR AGE

The first Christians appear not to have felt the need to build churches. At the beginning they were all Jews, and seem to have been satisfied with the facilities their old religion provided. They went to the Temple and kept the Jewish feasts. This was as much cultural as religious, it kept them part of the Jewish community. They also went to the synagogue, where the Law, the Prophets and the Writings were read and discussed. Some things they did in their homes. There they kept the memory of Jesus the Christ alive by re-enacting the Last Supper he had with his disciples. They had a common meal and taught that Jesus had told them to do this, and as they broke the bread they should remember his broken body, and as they poured the wine they should remember his shed blood. At those common meals, they pledged themselves to love one another and keep the teaching of Jesus. New converts were invited to these house meetings and taught the meaning of their faith – at first from people who had been with Jesus.

Two things changed that quite early:

First, the Christian community spread out from Jerusalem and into the Gentile world. This meant that there was no tradition of Jewish Temple worship, but there was much idol worship from which the new converts had to be set free. Something like Christian synagogues were needed for this. The "breaking of bread" would have to be learnt, some ceremony for baptism developed, and simple ethical teaching would be needed.

Second, the Temple in Jerusalem was destroyed in AD 70, and later all Jews were driven out of Jerusalem. The Jewish people themselves were now a wandering race, with the synagogue and the home forming the two centres of their religious life.

Jewish Christians at first joined in the same synagogue as the Jews but quarrels arose and they separated.

Early Gentile Worship

Paul and Barnabas were pioneers of a movement that must have involved many of the first Christians and probably some of the original disciples, who seem quickly to have been called apostles (meaning, sent out). The movement into the Gentile world raised acute problems. The Jews had a strict code of behaviour – they were the puritans of the ancient world – and an established form of worship which involved the whole Jewish community. When Christianity became the religion of groups of pagans they had no such inheritance. Paul's letters are full of instructions about how to behave, taken from his own tradition in Judaism. For instance, in their assemblies women should keep quiet and cover their heads. The re-enacting of the Last Supper was a great problem to Paul. In Judaism, he had the tradition of the Passover meal, and as a strict Pharisee he saw the religious content as dominant. The pagan tradition also had common meals, but they were great fun, parties, eating and drinking, often to excess, pouring libations to the gods, eating the meat sacrificed to them earlier, and a good deal of easy sexual relations. To a strict Jew, this would be shocking. To a pagan convert it seemed that the celebration of the Last Supper was the Christian form of their old feasts. At Corinth they made a party of it. Paul was shocked, and rounded on them for their desecration of this sacred meal. He then recited to them an early formula which he had learnt when he first became a Christian. One can see the value of such a formula in the early Gentile worship:

> For I received from the Lord what I also passed on to you: The Lord Jesus, on the night he was betrayed, took bread and when he had given thanks, he broke it and said, This is my body, which is for you; do this in remembrance of me. In the same manner, after supper he took the cup saying, This cup is the new covenant in my blood; do this whenever you drink it, in remembrance of me.
> For whenever you eat this bread and drink this cup, you proclaim the Lord's death until he comes.

Comments of a Roman Official

About fifty years later, at the beginning of the second century, an over-scrupulous Roman official sent by the Emperor Trajan to put in order the cities of Bithynia, reported what he had learnt of Christian worship there. Talk of eating flesh and drinking blood had led to rumours about the goings-on at Christian secret meetings. Pliny, the Roman official, arrested some Christians and frighened them, even using torture where necessary, so that they would fulfil the test applied to suspect Christians. This was to declare their loyalty to the Emperor by worshipping him, and at the same time, for good measure, cursing Christ. Some did this and from them he learnt what really went on at Christian meetings:

> They maintained that the amount of their fault or error had been this, that it was their habit on a fixed day to assemble before daylight and sing by turns a hymn to Christ as god; and that they bound themselves with an oath, not for any crime, but not to commit theft or

robbery or adultery, not to break their word, and not to deny a deposit when demanded. After this was done, their custom was to depart, and meet together again to take food, but ordinary and harmless food; and even this (they said) they had given up after the issue of my edict, by which in accordance with your commands I had forbidden the existence of clubs.

Pliny found nothing wrong, except "wicked and arrogant superstition". But he is worried about the growth of this superstition:

The matter seemed to me to be worth deliberation, especially on account of those in danger; for many of all ages and every rank, and even both sexes, are brought into present or future danger. The contagion of that superstition has penetrated not the cities only, but the villages and country; yet it seems possible to stop it and set it right.

The reason Pliny gives for his optimism shows that the incursion on pagan worship had been considerable, but was now halted:

At any rate it is certain enough that the almost deserted temples begin to be resorted to, that long disused ceremonies of religion are restored, and that fodder for victims finds a market, whereas buyers till now were very few. From this it may easily be supposed, what a multitude of men can be reclaimed, if there be a place of repentance.

That was the situation, and even the Book of the Revelation in the New Testament confirms it. There, letters to seven churches reveal a picture of decline after considerable advance. Pliny and men like him regarded this sect of Christians as one of the many mystery religions which were sweeping in to Rome and the Empire from the East. They mostly had baptism, secret ceremonies, talk of blood and very close fellowship. The Christians must have seemed similar. The response of the authorities was a tough line with illegal or harmful sects. The Christians called this persecution. During the first onslaught the Church declined, and then during the period of calm grew again.

Justin Martyr

Another fifty years on from Pliny, a Christian writer described worship in the middle of the second century. As he wrote from the inside he was better informed than the Roman official. Justin, a philosopher, who was born about AD 100, was converted to Christianity by an old man he met on the seashore at Ephesus. He continued to wear the philosopher's cloak and taught in Rome. Eventually he suffered martyrdom in a persecution when he was about sixty. He tried to explain to Jews and pagans what Christianity was about, and gave an account of Christian worship. First a description of Baptism:

As many as are persuaded and believe that things are true which are taught by us, and said to be true and promise that they can live accordingly – they are taught to pray and to ask God, with fasting, forgiveness of their sins, and we pray and fast together with them. Then they are brought by us to a place where there is water, and born again with a new birth even as we ourselves were born again. For in the name of God the Father and Lord of the universe, and of our Saviour Jesus Christ and the Holy Spirit do they

receive the washing in water. For Christ said, "Except
ye be born again, ye shall not enter into the kingdom of
heaven".

After the baptism, the newly "enlightened", as Justin calls
them, are taken to the other brethren where they join with
them in prayers:

> We salute each other with a kiss when our prayers are
> over. Afterwards is brought to the president of the
> brethren bread and a cup of water and wine, and he
> takes it and offers up praise and glory to the Father of
> the universe through the name of the Son and Holy
> Spirit, and gives thanks at length, that we have
> received these favours from him; and at the end of his
> prayers and thanksgiving the whole people present
> responds, saying, Amen. Then ... the deacons ... allow
> every one of those present to partake of the bread and
> wine and water for which thanks have been given; and
> for those absent they take away a portion.

Justin continued by explaining that this is called, *Eucharist*
and adds.

> It is not lawful for any man to partake of it but he who
> believes our teaching to be true, and has been washed
> with the washing, which is the forgiveness of sins and
> unto a new birth, and is for living as Christ
> commanded. For the Apostles in the memoirs which
> they composed, which are called gospels, thus
> delivered that command which was given them – that
> Jesus took bread and gave thanks and said, This do in
> remembrance of me, this is my body; and likewise he
> took the cup, and after he had given thanks said, This

is my blood, and gave it to them.

Justin explained that the Christians discuss these matters; "the wealthy also give of their abundance" to help those in need. They are often together and when they eat they always say grace, thanking the Maker of all through his Son, Jesus Christ and the Holy Spirit.

Justin also explained that they meet on Sundays and that

> The memoirs of the Apostles or the writings of the prophets are read as long as time allows. After the reading, the president gives his explanation [this is obviously what we would call the sermon]. Then they rise, pray and the Eucharist begins – bread is brought and wine and water. A collection is taken after the Eucharist and it is given to the president, and he it is that succours orphans and widows, and those that are in want through sickness or any other cause, and those that are in bonds, and the strangers that are sojourning, and in short he has the care of all that are in need.

Justin also explained the reason for meeting on Sunday, instead of Saturday.

> Sunday is the day when God changed the darkness and matter in his making of the world, and Jesus Christ our Saviour on the same day rose from the dead.

The Last Supper and the memory of the death of Christ thus dominated the early worship, and the day on which they met reminded them of the resurrection. Their guide was the gospels and other apostolic writings.

The New Testament

Not long after Justin, steps were taken to form a Canon (an accepted body of texts) of the New Testament, closely modelled on the structure of the Jewish Scripture, which was now called the Old Testament. The Old Testament remained as holy, containing laws of conduct, teaching and promises of Christ.

The New Testament was intended to be the writings by the apostles or by those who had known the apostles. Every book, chosen from a wide variety of writings, had to be associated with an apostle, i.e. one of the Twelve disciples, or such an apostle as Paul.

The Four Gospels, chosen no doubt from many, were all thought to be associated with one of the disciples: Matthew, Mark (from Peter), Luke (from Paul), and John. They were comparable with the *Torah*, or five books of Moses. After these, just as Joshua continues the story of the *Torah*, the Acts of the Apostles continues the story of the gospels.

The letters which follow, like the Prophets of the Old Testament, explain the meaning of the gospels. They are mostly by Paul and were preserved because the churches to which they were addressed found them helpful.

The Book of Revelation is the only parallel to the other books of the Hebrew Bible.

There was much discussion about the composition of the New Testament, but once its canon was established it became sacred, and played a vital part in worship. During the period of fierce persecution which followed in the third and early fourth century, the Scriptures were guarded by deacons, who endured torture and faced death rather than surrender them to the persecutors. The Roman officials soon discovered that the Bible played so vital a part in the life of the Christians, that they thought to destroy Christianity by destroying its books.

The Age of Constantine

The years of bitter persecution were followed by a period of power. The Emperor embraced Christianity, although he was not baptized until his dying moments. The change was abrupt. Thousands poured into the Church of the Emperor. Time-servers rubbed shoulders with the children of the martyrs.

The Church divided into two emphases. Those disgusted by the wealth and superficiality of the new Christians, separated themselves from the world into a monastic movement. Worship dominated their lives and they concentrated their minds on holy things. They renounced the world, but prayed for it. The other emphasis was shown by those who sought to Christianize the Empire. They now persecuted the pagans, pulled down the temples or renovated them as churches. Christianity as the conquering religion acquired a very different character. The monks went on trying to retain the original teaching and spirit. One of them, helped of course by others, spent his life working on the Bible and translating it from the Hebrew and Greek, which was no longer understood, into the common Latin of the day. Jerome's translation of the Bible was known as the Vulgate (i.e. for the people). Constantine hoped that the Church would hold his empire together. He favoured it and built churches of magnificence. Worship became grander and far removed from the simplicity of the home or house church. The Christians came out of the catacombs into the palaces.

All the warnings that Jesus obviously gave to his disciples that they would be persecuted, hated, unpopular seemed ridiculous now that the Church had conquered the world.

The Upper Room where the Last Supper had been held bore some resemblance to the room where the earliest Christians broke bread together; but now, the splendour of the Mass seemed ages removed. There was more wealth on one altar than Jesus had handled in his life. The successors of Peter and John could no longer say to the beggar at the gate of the Temple, "Silver and gold have I none", but with that wealth something was lost. They could also no longer say, "In the name of Jesus of Nazareth, rise up and walk".

The Power of the Church

The fall of the Empire, the spread of Christianity triumphantly over Europe, the wealth and influence even of the monasteries, and the power of the priests shed darkness over a medieval Europe. The Church acquired power over the people. Worship was led by priests, and the people were observers. The Bible was in Latin, as the languages of Europe became the language of the people. There was resistance to translating the Bible into these languages because the Bible was not meant to be for the people, but to be interpreted by the Church. A priest was seen as having a special grace to understand the Bible. He therefore was God's spokesman.

The Last Supper, which had been an element in Christian worship from the beginning, became a mystery in which the priest had power to transform the bread into the body of Christ. This he could dispense or withhold as though he were giving or withholding salvation. The people were in tutelage to the Church, and for the forgiveness which Christ had freely offered, they depended upon the absolution of the priest. With such power, the Church became corrupt, and the priests often abused their powers. Bishops became princes with secular power and sometimes even with armies. The shadow of the Galilean was faint.

The Morning Star of the Reformation

In the fourteenth century, when the Plague had swept across Europe, decimating the population of the continent and of England, there was unrest in many countries. In England, John Wycliffe sympathized with the plight of the impoverished people and, although he did not support the Peasants' Revolt, he could understand its reasons. He saw the hold that priests and preaching friars had over the people. Worship had become a means of control, from the Confessional to the Mass. The friars could threaten with the Word of God, and no one could challenge them because the Bible was a closed book. John Wycliffe, who is in many ways the source of the Reformation in England, saw two abuses and acted. The one was the closed book, and he set out to translate the Bible from its hidden Latin into the language of the people. The other was the Mass, and he attacked the superstitious attitude which gave magical powers to the priests. The friars were faced with an opposition by his Lollard preachers, who came in their poverty to speak to poor people and used the English version of the Bible which all could understand. The power of the Church suppressed him, and his English Bibles were burned, his preachers hunted down. But he had left a memory of free worship and an open Bible.

The Reformation of England

The centuries of religious strife that followed left Europe divided between Catholic and Protestant. The story is a long and complicated one, and neither side came off very well. It need not be told here. England gained from the strife an open Bible, a Book of Common Prayer in English, a clergy much nearer to the people because of their involvement in the everyday problems of family life. England lost the monasteries. The Church was much more involved in the political life of the nation, with the King supreme under Christ rather than the Pope. We acquired a national church. There were those, however, who felt that the reform had not gone far enough. They tried to remove all the ceremony from the churches and concentrate upon consideration of God's Word.

England has retained this mix of Catholic and Reformed. The many denominations have confused the picture a bit, but there is no mistaking the different patterns of worship in Catholic, Anglican and Free Church. All three have changed and grown closer to each other. The various patterns include: the ceremony of the Mass, now largely in English even in Roman Catholic churches, reading of Scripture, Prayers, Hymns and the sense of fellowship among worshippers. Baptism has continued, but with variations – the Baptists baptize believers only, and the different denominations interpret what happens at baptism differently. The growth of the ecumenical movement has led to a greater understanding of one another's traditions, and even a borrowing from one another. The worship of all churches has been reformed and changed to a considerable degree over the past century and a half. In the nineteenth century, many Catholic practices were reintroduced in Church of England worship; the Free Churches put added emphasis on preaching, but in this century they have learnt much about formal worship from other traditions. The Roman Catholic Church has seen considerable change this century also: a biblical renewal, the participation of the laity in worship and, with the Second Vatican Council, worship in the vernacular.

Hymns have also changed this century, with many hymnbook revisions or new editions, including several new hymns and new tunes. The Church of England has attempted to replace the Book of Common Prayer with the *Alternative Service Book, 1980*. Considerable as these changes have been, they consist largely of adaptation.

The Charismatic Movement, however, has introduced a totally new form of worship. It is spontaneous , spirit-led in a way that appears to an outsider as uncontrolled, and including some primitive elements like speaking with tongues, singing and praying in ecstasy. This charismatic movement has led to extensive healing services, even in those congregations which otherwise show no sign of charismatic influence.

The Extent of our Inheritance

Before we turn to the main purpose of this chapter, which is the place of worship in a secular society, we need to note what has been inherited from the past, how much is essential to worship and how much is disposable baggage.

It would appear that those who are believers need to meet for some kind of fellowship which is determined by their belief. From what we said in the previous chapter about the "waywardness of the Holy Spirit", it is clear that this fellowship is the work of the Holy Spirit and that therefore its form is unpredictable.

An intense fellowship excludes; an open fellowship tends to lose its identity. There needs to be in this meeting of believers a definiteness, but also an openness to others who are not, or not yet, believers. The balance is maintained, not by the Holy Spirit, but by the attitude of mind of the believers. Thus a congregation may decide to continue its traditional practices for the sake of preserving the "mysteries"; or it may adapt its worship to become intelligible to non-believers. Things are not quite as clear cut as that may appear. The essential traditions may be matters of dispute – how far is a worshipping congregation committed to the Lord's Prayer, the Creeds, the reading almost exclusively from the Bible (and perhaps commitment to a particular translation), the Psalms, hymns of a particular type with familiar tunes, prayers of a certain style, an ecclesiastical building, an authentic priesthood, a liturgy and preaching? Every element in that list needs careful discussion. I have not included the much larger issue of the Eucharist, which in one form or another is accepted as essential by almost all the various traditions of Christianity. Equally, I have not included Baptism.

The Lord's Prayer

Two of the gospels (Matthew and Luke) include an account of Jesus being asked by his disciples for help in prayer. His reply is, "This is how you should pray" or "When you pray say", with a prayer which in the two gospels differs only slightly. The Church has traditionally concluded that the words of the Lord's Prayer should be used. But it is a very compact prayer and not at all obvious in its meaning. The result is that constant repetition dulls the sense of the prayer, and few who pray it think much about what it means. Surely Jesus could not have meant such repetition. It would be against his general teaching about prayer, where he condemned "vain repetitions".

So, in a secular age when prayer is not presumed to have magical qualities, we should look more closely at what Jesus did say to his disciples. He gave them a model prayer, which seems to have been used as such by many early Christian writers. The prayer lists the ways in which we may approach

God – or rather, the way in which the disciples may approach God. For it is surely possible that some of these approaches are linked to the thinking of the time. Let us take them one by one.

Our Father who art in heaven hallowed be thy name. That at once conjures up Freud's accusation that God is an illusion, a substitute for a father whom we discovered in our childhood to have feet of clay. It also raises questions about Christianity (like Judaism and Islam) being a male-dominated religion. With so many one-parent families, what can the concept of God as a father mean other than the one who deserts? In the stability of Jewish family life and the first-century acceptance of male supremacy, "Father" was a good name for God. Even as early as the fourteenth century, Julian of Norwich can address God as father and mother, the continuing usefulness of "Father" alone being called in question. Perhaps in this age we should approach God as Sustainer of the Universe. That would more readily embrace the following phrase, "who art in heaven", which is even more difficult in a secular society with a scientific world view.

Thy kingdom come. This is a prayer for the rule of God to be established in the world. The word "kingdom" is outdated and even misleading. The following clause, **Thy will be done**, is clearer and says exactly the same thing. A prayer for the Sustainer of the Universe to be in control is fully understood in a secular society. Some will, of course, interpret that as a plea for the proper operation of the laws of nature. A prayer that the Sustainer of the Universe may be in control is mythological, but clear. The widespread concern about the environment, and the threat to the existence of our planet makes such a prayer meaningful, except that you must decide whom you are addressing. As believers we are addressing God, but there is no reason why we should entangle him in the mythology of the first-century Judaism. That dispenses with the clause, **on earth as it is in heaven**. **Give us this day our daily bread**. Few who are hungry or suffering from malnutrition would find that prayer difficult to understand. For in the more affluent parts of the world, it may appear to be addressed to the wrong person. It is not God but humanity which is now responsible for feeding the world. Our prayers in Europe should be for ourselves and for our systems, not so much to be fed as to be used responsibly.

This would link closely with the next petition, **Forgive us our trespasses**. In this way the prayer makes a deal of sense if used as a model prayer, rather than its words being taken as sacrosanct. We have so far prayed for the proper use of the environment, the just distribution of the resources of the earth, according to need rather than possession, and now forgiveness that we have so misused environment and resources.

Coupling that petition for forgiveness with, **as we forgive those who trespass against us**, leads us to consider our own unforgiving attitude to those who, in their desperation, use violence against us, or those who resort to crime when they see affluence inaccessible around them. If we need forgiveness for not distributing justly the resources of the world, we may forgive the shop-lifter or even the terrorist.

In this kind of context, **Lead us not into temptation, but deliver us from evil** requires no modification. It is the desperate cry of one who finds that the system which sustains him compels him to do wrong by his fellow man, whether by violence or by lack of compassion.
For thine is the kingdom, the power and the glory is part of the doxology which acknowledges the Sustaining power of the Universe.

I am not suggesting that we rewrite the Lord's Prayer, but that we use it in a way that is intelligible to our age, and do not exclude those whose world is secular (and what else should a world be but secular?), whether they are believers or not. For the effort to match our worship to thought patterns of the age keeps worshippers from becoming schizophrenic, thinking one way in church and another in the real world.

The Creeds

As a convenient summary of the principal tenets of the Christian Faith the creeds can be useful. They proved powerful in Nazi Germany as an affirmation of the faith against the perversions of the German Christians (Christians who collaborated with Hitler's régime). But they had to be brought up to date with the Barmen Declaration, in which the Confessing Church related faith to the circumstances of the day. Creeds can also be a hindrance. They dogmatize belief and are often simply repeated. All of them arose in connection with some specific situation, and when that situation changes it is dangerous to give them eternal significance as though they were absolute. At first, a creed was a convenient summary for newly baptized Christians, a guide to the basic elements of the Christian preaching. More elaborate creeds were devised to assure that Christians did not fall into heresy. The history of the Councils and the Creeds that emerged from them is not a happy one. Instead of useful summaries, which need to be updated, they became tests to determine orthodoxy. Those who did not accept them were condemned, and after the age of Constantine that could mean death. They have survived in our worship rather like fossils, reminders of living issues of long ago. Some of the statements in the creed recited during worship are not understood, others are not believed. In a modern society it is probably good to rewrite them or to be clear about their status. What we have done with the phrases of the Lord's

Prayer could certainly be done with profit for the creeds. If worship in a secular society needs a clear statement of what is believed by those worshipping, the ancient creeds will not do. But if new creeds are written for worship they must be understood as temporary, not binding subsequent generations as the ancient creeds have bound us.

The Exclusive Use of the Bible

The second century felt the need for an authentic selection of its literature, and gave to the New Testament the kind of authority that the Jews gave to the Old Testament. Yet the Bible is a collection of writings of different kinds and cannot have the same authority throughout. Modern criticism has compelled us to read the Bible historically, and when this has been done in a positive way it is enlightening. Its authority still rests in the original criterion: all the writings are in some way connected with the original witness of the disciples to Jesus the Christ, whom they knew as Jesus of Nazareth. It would seem unwise to give to later literature the same standing. Apart from anything else, there would be no end to it. The more we move away from the original sources, the more tenuous our statements become. This is not to ascribe any magic quality to the Bible, which can be criticized like any other book; but it does mean that the constant reading of literature written so close to the events of the Incarnation keeps the worshippers acquainted with the basic witness.

That does not mean that other helpful literature should not be read in church, but it should be clear what we are reading. Preaching has long made use of poetry and other writings to elucidate a point, and a service of worship can be made interesting and instructive by the reading of selected passages by modern writers or classical texts from all ages. Christians have not followed the practice of the Greek-speaking Jews in Alexandria, who once they had translated the accepted books of their Bible added a few more in the Greek. These additional books are usually printed as The Apocrypha.

The New Testament remained intact. The Catholic Church at the Council of Trent (1542) defined the official translation into Latin as the authorized version. Since then Catholics and Protestants have had many modern translations, in many languages. This century has seen a plethora of modern translations in English, the reading of which makes the text more intelligible, and its relevance is therefore more easily accepted. But there are some who consider that the modern translation takes away the aura of Scripture. There is no doubt that there is an evocative effect when ancient translations of well-known passages are read.

Hymn Singing

It is almost a universal tendency for any group that gathers frequently, and is united in a common purpose, to sing. A football crowd has its song, sometimes a hymn which may seem quite irrevelant – "Abide with me" at Cup Finals; "Guide me, O Thou Great Jehovah" at Welsh Rugby Internationals; "The Saints come marching in"; "I'm forever blowing bubbles", and other signature tunes of football teams. Revolutionary groups also find that a song is needed to lift up their common purpose – "We shall overcome, one day", and of course, the Marseillaise.

It is not surprising, therefore, that from the earliest days Christians have sung – at first the Jewish Psalms, with Christian interpretation, and then more songs of Christian origin. A few are in the New Testament – "My soul doth magnify the Lord" (Mary's song of praise), *Nunc Dimittis* (Simeon's prayer after seeing the Christ child) and several others. The *Te Deum*, which comes from the time of Ambrose in the fourth century, is an early hymn. Every age produces its own special hymns – of praise to God, of Christian beliefs, of encouragement, of repentance, of prayer, etc. In this century, new hymnbooks have been produced every few years, some mixing up new hymns with favourite old ones. Often the tunes are more important than the words! A deliberate attempt has been made more recently to write hymns of topical relevance, that lift a congregation out of the nostalgia of ancient and sacred words to recall the issues in the world of today. One good example of relating the words to a scientific world is a hymn by David Harding, published in *New Life* in 1971 and subsequently included in many collections of modern hymns: "God of receding matter". The hymn continues with praise to the God of "light years", "stars diverse", "majestic mountains", "mellowed landscapes" and of "human feelings".

Some of the new hymns are also prayers. One from *Thank you Music*, published in 1975, written by J. Hewer, is a prayer sung:

Father I place into your hands
The things that I can't do.

In different verses the hymn lists "the things": "the times that I've been through", "the way that I should go", "friends and family", "the things that trouble me", etc. The last line is always "for I know I always can trust you". It is a hymn of trust in God, using the image of "Father", and prayer for closer association with God. These hymns of the seventies are no longer new, but some will survive as year by year more new hymns are written.

But perhaps more significant than the change of words has been the great variety of music used. Each generation has taken popular music of the day and enabled new generations to express their solidarity in song. Particularly for young people it becomes necessary to have in church the music which is meaningful to their generation. This place given to music has often meant the neglect or minimizing of the importance of the words. The style of secular songs, which for some time now has been repetitive rather than narrative, has come to our hymnbooks too. The music predominates and the words are repeated like a *mantra*. Sometimes a psalm is remoulded, and even Latin phrases used for their sound. A good example, dependent upon its music, is the version of Psalm 100 by Fred Dunn, from *Thank you Music*:

> Jubilate, ev'rybody,
> Serve the Lord in all your ways.

Such a hymn may be sung again and again. It requires no further verses, just repetition.

It must be said that not all congregations readily accept this new style in words and music. Congregations largely of young people eagerly sing these modern hymns because of their relevance and nearness to the culture in which they live. Older people may receive them with equal enthusiasm, livening a worship which had become routine. There are others for whom the older words and music bear the weight of their experience, and they have a love which cannot be shared with alien art forms. The future, however, seems to lie with a mixture, in which old established hymns will retain their place for what they have meant in the past and still mean to an older generation, but with the steady addition of new hymns and new music as the secular culture grows. In his day, even Mozart's "Vespers" were considered too innovative by many!

Public Prayer
A worshipping community may be gathered by song, but

prayer has always been the acceptable approach to God. It is born in private communion with God, but has had its place from the beginning in the worship of the group. Luke writes in the Acts of the Apostles, after the excitement of the Day of Pentecost, that the newly enlarged Christian Church, disciples and converts together, "devoted themselves to the apostles' teaching and to the fellowship, to the breaking of bread *and to prayer*".

We have looked at the Lord's Prayer, but other prayers have become familiar from Prayer Books and constant use. Even so-called "extempore prayer" has tended to fall into certain acceptable phrases. A congregation familiar with this may go on using it long after the language in everyday speech is changed. An example is the use of "Thou" well after it had fallen out of use in common speech. Words that have changed their meaning are still used in prayers with the old meaning – "prevent" is a good example, for it once meant "to go before". The last forty or fifty years have seen a rewriting of such prayers as in the Anglican *Alternative Service Book,* 1980, and in collections of "Contemporary Prayers". This has often been more than rewriting old prayers. A prayer for Advent by Jamie Wallace in his *There's a Time and Place*, is headed "Prayer of suppressed excitement"

God and Father of us all:
we thank you for this exciting time of year.
Parcels are wrapped and hidden, secrets are kept,
good things are cooked in the kitchen and stored in the
freezer ready for the Christmas feast.
It is time for looking foward,
hastening the day, but spinning out the fun of
    preparation.
The eyes of parents and grandparents light up
with the glee they see in the children.

Lord, help the children to hold and hallow the wonder
  they feel,
this magic which is pure and undefiled because it is
  yours,
because it speaks the story of your love
and is always true.

Lord, keep us who are older aware of the wonder too;
quicken our senses if they have been dulled
with business and greed and comfort and worry – and
  age;
so that we too may know again the desire, the
  impatience and
the joy of Christmas.

Ancient prayers are modernized, and modern prayers are
written so that the whole congregation may be gathered in to
share the prayers uttered by the person presiding. Even
then, there is a danger that the president is up there praying
while the people are listening, trying to feel what he feels.
More is needed than modern words and concepts. The need
for involvement of all people has been increasingly felt. This
may be done by a group from the congregation coming
forward and taking the prayers between them. More
drastically, it may be done by asking the congregation to
voice their prayer needs. The presiding person may ask what
should be prayed for, and as requests come from several of
the people, gather them up in a prayer request to God.

There can be no worship unless there is a realization of the
presence of God, and that makes worship in a secular society
difficult. Prayer must have an address, but it can involve the
secular world, and those who cannot believe can at least see
that there are people who do believe and that what they are

praying for is part of their secular world.

An Ecclesiastical Building

The power and splendour of the Church expresses itself in magnificent structures. As George MacLeod used to say, "The Gothic Cathedrals shot up all over Europe, like a flight of arrows". At a later time, there were those who sought simplicity and insisted that their churches should be as plain as possible. Endangered minorities built unobtrusive buildings. Then, that very puritan tradition which has insisted upon barn-like structures grew rich and powerful – the merchants of London and the mill-owners of the north – and tried at times to imitate the ancient glory or the modern Anglican Gothic. In the age of competition, Free Churches wished to be as good as the Anglicans. Sometimes the churches were built in memory of God and to the glory of the benefactor. Some, of course, were built the way they were for the services of the church. A cathedral had ceremonies to perform which required the space and splendour of the ancient gothic. A popular Free Church with regular congregations of more than two thousand needed a large auditorium. But for a very long time the Church existed without special buildings. There has been a steady recognition that the lovely old churches are no longer suitable for the activity of a modern church.

In fact, many large, old churches were bombed during the Second World War, and quite different buildings were put up in their place. The steady decline of congregations since the First World War has required much smaller auditoria for the Free Churches, whose ceremonies do not usually require the space and splendour of a cathedral. In that period of decline in worship, many churches have found their witness to their faith is more effective in organizations, bringing natural groupings of lonely people, or training the young for life, or providing activities for unemployed and retired, than in repeated church services. Worship has continued, but most churches use their ''premises'' more than they use their ''churches''.

Worship is not the only service a church offers. It serves the community in its need, creates fellowship, demonstrates a way of life, and is present in the community ''for others''.

An Authentic Priesthood
Every tradition within the Church has developed its own conception of the priesthood – derived from the Old Testament rather than from the pagan mysteries. Some have stressed the need for a direct link with the original apostles . The priest is then a special person – usually male – who has received grace from a bishop, who stands in the line of succession which links him with the apostles. Others have stressed the personal call of God to the ministry, even those who call them by such names as ''clerk to the meeting''. Someone has to organize the events that happen in a church or meeting place. The extent to which this person is separated from the outside community depends upon the way in which his or her activities are distinguished as priestly activity in the church services, and spiritual direction, on the one hand; and service to the community, on the other. All priests and ministers serve the community, and it is for that reason that their houses had tax concessions. But how different are they from social workers? The answer must lie in the church activities. In some Free Church traditions, the minister is a person set apart for specific duties. He is no different from any other member of the church, except that the church supports him so that he can be set free to deal with specifically church matters. In the Catholic tradition he is different from the laity by his ordination, the grace given

him to function as a priest. For this reason the decision as to whether or not to ordain women to the priesthood is a serious decision. After centuries of male priests it is a major decision to ordain women. In the Free Churches the acceptance of women ministers has no difficulty except prejudice. There are many things in the Catholic tradition which only a priest can do. Principal among them is the celebration of the Eucharist.

The Mysteries

"Breaking of Bread" is as old as prayer in the Christian Church. It is a mystery which few churches have abandoned, even though some have neglected it. This lies at the heart of Christian worship and has to be preserved. It will not yield to secular interpretation. In its long history, the various parts of the Christian Church have quarrelled over its meaning, but none have explained its abiding importance. Behind every theory the words "Do this in remembrance of me" are heard. The Eucharist remains to be done, not explained.

It is reasonable to expect Christians to talk a contemporary language, and for that the older translations of the Bible are put into modern English, the prayers are contemporary, the music of the age, the hymns concerned with the issues of the day. All this is because Christian worship is inclusive, not exclusive. The message of the Christian Church to the world, whether in the proclamation of the Gospel or commenting upon contemporary issues, must not be in a secret language. To a large extent this modernizing of worship is being accomplished – however slowly! Some of the great religious words are hardly used now – salvation, repentance, sin, conversion, redemption, etc. – except by a minority group of Christians and for the convenience of theologians. This is because we are only in process of discovering what they mean in our day.

The Eucharist, however, is different. This is private, not secret, but "family". We are happy that others should observe, but not change it. We are not fully aware of all it means, but we know that is is an act of obedience. It is celebrated as closely as possible to the original intention of our Lord, who said, "Do this!" It is for those who believe. Yet in some strange way, it proclaims the Gospel. When Paul repeated to the Corinthian Christians what he had learnt about the details of the Last Supper, he added: "For whenever you eat this bread and drink this cup, you proclaim the Lord's death until he comes." And so it has proved, whether in the Mass or the Eucharist, Holy Communion or the Lord's Supper, simple Communion or breaking of bread. The faith of those who partake is strengthened, and those who observe are often strangely moved at the power of this symbolic meal which gives assurance to believers.

When, after much debate in the BBC, shortly after the end of the Second World War, it was decided to lift the ban on the broadcasting of the Communion Service, the purpose was to serve the housebound and educate those whose experience was confined to one tradition; but it soon became clear that the broadcast presented the Christian message more powerfully to some listeners than the sermons ever did.

While worship changes, to meet the demands of a new age, there remains at its heart an act of obedience which does not change.

This can also be said to be true of Baptism, the gateway to the mysteries.

*   *   *

Into the Future
If all the churches should become museums, as many did in

the Soviet Union, or Supermarkets, which are perhaps the proper successors to our chapels in a consumer society, or Hindu Temples or Mosques, for more religious races, there would still be a community of Christians spread throughout society – as they were in the days of the Roman Empire.

They would appear in every walk of life with a sense of freedom, because they were confident that it was God's world. They would be at peace even in stressful circumstances. They would love one another and even their enemies. Having no churches to maintain, no hierarchy to support, they would be able to be generous and have time for compassion. They would be found where people were in need or frightened or depressed. They would be able to listen, because they were not hurrying to a meeting, nor anxious to be in time for church service. Somewhere they would meet, probably in their homes, to remember their crucified Lord and do what he had commanded, eating the bread and drinking the wine, knowing that he was with them and that he had died for them, and expecting his return.

Those who joined them would be taught the Christian way, and be baptized to mark their change of life. They would bring up their children with love, and care for those who had lost their parents. Orphans and widows would be their special concern. They would rejoice at young people discovering life and learning how to love, developing their skills and taking responsibility in the world. They would care for the aged, and visit them with comfort and encouragement. They would make the aged feel that they mattered. They would be with the dying, accompanying them to the gates of death with confidence in their Lord to take the hand that they had relinquished. They would hear the voice of their Lord in difficult times, saying, ''Take heart! I have overcome the world''.

It was something like that in the days of Tertullian in the

second century. We cannot, of course, go back to an earlier age; but we could catch its spirit of freedom. We are burdened with the guilt of two thousand years and enriched by the achievements of that same period. We have to carry the one as a burden of responsibility for the world, and discover the other as resources for the new adventure into the future.

Cardinal Suenens, who has guided the charismatic movement in the Roman Catholic Church with care and love, may be allowed to have the last word:

> Who would dare to say that the love and imagination
> of God were exhausted?
> To hope is a duty, not a luxury. To hope is not to
>   dream, but to turn dreams into reality.
> Happy are those who dream dreams and are ready to
>   pay the price to make them come true.